OPPOSING
VIEWPOINTS®
SERIES

Ethics

Other Books of Related Interest:

Opposing Viewpoints Series
Corporate Social Responsibility
Medical Testing
Performance-Enhancing Drugs
Whistleblowers

At Issue Series
Is Society Becoming Less Civil?
Negative Campaigning
The Right to Die

Current Controversies Series
Animal Rights
Media Ethics
Medical Ethics
US Government Corruption

"Congress shall make no law ... abridging the freedom of speech, or of the press."

First Amendment to the US Constitution

The basic foundation of our democracy is the First Amendment guarantee of freedom of expression. The Opposing Viewpoints series is dedicated to the concept of this basic freedom and the idea that it is more important to practice it than to enshrine it.

OPPOSING VIEWPOINTS® SERIES

I Ethics

Noël Merino, Book Editor

GREENHAVEN PRESS
A part of Gale, Cengage Learning

GALE
CENGAGE Learning·

Farmington Hills, Mich • San Francisco • New York • Waterville, Maine
Meriden, Conn • Mason, Ohio • Chicago

Patricia Coryell, *Vice President & Publisher, New Products & GVRL*
Douglas Dentino, *Manager, New Products*
Judy Galens, *Acquisitions Editor*

© 2015 Greenhaven Press, a part of Gale, Cengage Learning.

WCN: 01-100-101

Gale and Greenhaven Press are registered trademarks used herein under license.

For more information, contact:
Greenhaven Press
27500 Drake Rd.
Farmington Hills, MI 48331-3535
Or you can visit our Internet site at gale.cengage.com

For product information and technology assistance, contact us at

Gale Customer Support, 1-800-877-4253
For permission to use material from this text or product, submit all requests online at www.cengage.com/permissions

Further permissions questions can be emailed to permissionrequest@cengage.com

Articles in Greenhaven Press anthologies are often edited for length to meet page requirements. In addition, original titles of these works are changed to clearly present the main thesis and to explicitly indicate the author's opinion. Every effort is made to ensure that Greenhaven Press accurately reflects the original intent of the authors. Every effort has been made to trace the owners of copyrighted material.

Cover Image copyright © xtock/Shutterstock.com.

LIBRARY OF CONGRESS CATALOGING-IN-PUBLICATION DATA

Ethics / Noël Merino, book editor.
    pages cm. -- -- (Opposing viewpoints) Summary: "Opposing Viewpoints is the leading source for libraries and classrooms in need of current-issue materials. The viewpoints are selected from a wide range of highly respected sources and publications"-- Provided by publisher.
    Includes bibliographical references and index.
    ISBN 978-0-7377-7260-9 (hardback) -- ISBN 978-0-7377-7261-6 (paperback)
    1. Ethics--Juvenile literature. 2. Values--Juvenile literature. I. Merino, Noël, editor.
    BJ1012.E8864 2015
    170--dc23
                                                                    2014029440

Printed in the United States of America
1 2 3 4 5 6 7 18 17 16 15 14

Contents

Chapter 3: Should Religious Beliefs About Ethics Justify Behavior?

Chapter 4: How Should Ethics Guide Economic Policies?

Why Consider Opposing Viewpoints?

> *"The only way in which a human being can make some approach to knowing the whole of a subject is by hearing what can be said about it by persons of every variety of opinion and studying all modes in which it can be looked at by every character of mind. No wise man ever acquired his wisdom in any mode but this."*
>
> *John Stuart Mill*

In our media-intensive culture it is not difficult to find differing opinions. Thousands of newspapers and magazines and dozens of radio and television talk shows resound with differing points of view. The difficulty lies in deciding which opinion to agree with and which "experts" seem the most credible. The more inundated we become with differing opinions and claims, the more essential it is to hone critical reading and thinking skills to evaluate these ideas. Opposing Viewpoints books address this problem directly by presenting stimulating debates that can be used to enhance and teach these skills. The varied opinions contained in each book examine many different aspects of a single issue. While examining these conveniently edited opposing views, readers can develop critical thinking skills such as the ability to compare and contrast authors' credibility, facts, argumentation styles, use of persuasive techniques, and other stylistic tools. In short, the Opposing Viewpoints Series is an ideal way to attain the higher-level thinking and reading skills so essential in a culture of diverse and contradictory opinions.

In addition to providing a tool for critical thinking, Opposing Viewpoints books challenge readers to question their own strongly held opinions and assumptions. Most people form their opinions on the basis of upbringing, peer pressure, and personal, cultural, or professional bias. By reading carefully balanced opposing views, readers must directly confront new ideas as well as the opinions of those with whom they disagree. This is not to argue simplistically that everyone who reads opposing views will—or should—change his or her opinion. Instead, the series enhances readers' understanding of their own views by encouraging confrontation with opposing ideas. Careful examination of others' views can lead to the readers' understanding of the logical inconsistencies in their own opinions, perspective on why they hold an opinion, and the consideration of the possibility that their opinion requires further evaluation.

Evaluating Other Opinions

To ensure that this type of examination occurs, Opposing Viewpoints books present all types of opinions. Prominent spokespeople on different sides of each issue as well as well-known professionals from many disciplines challenge the reader. An additional goal of the series is to provide a forum for other, less known, or even unpopular viewpoints. The opinion of an ordinary person who has had to make the decision to cut off life support from a terminally ill relative, for example, may be just as valuable and provide just as much insight as a medical ethicist's professional opinion. The editors have two additional purposes in including these less known views. One, the editors encourage readers to respect others' opinions—even when not enhanced by professional credibility. It is only by reading or listening to and objectively evaluating others' ideas that one can determine whether they are worthy of consideration. Two, the inclusion of such viewpoints encourages the important critical thinking skill of objectively evaluating an author's credentials and bias. This evaluation will illuminate an author's reasons for taking a particular stance on an issue and will aid in readers' evaluation of the author's ideas.

It is our hope that these books will give readers a deeper understanding of the issues debated and an appreciation of the complexity of even seemingly simple issues when good and honest people disagree. This awareness is particularly important in a democratic society such as ours in which people enter into public debate to determine the common good. Those with whom one disagrees should not be regarded as enemies but rather as people whose views deserve careful examination and may shed light on one's own.

Thomas Jefferson once said that "difference of opinion leads to inquiry, and inquiry to truth." Jefferson, a broadly educated man, argued that "if a nation expects to be ignorant and free . . . it expects what never was and never will be." As individuals and as a nation, it is imperative that we consider the opinions of others and examine them with skill and discernment. The Opposing Viewpoints series is intended to help readers achieve this goal.

David L. Bender and Bruno Leone,
Founders

Introduction

"I consider ethics to be an exclusively human concern with no superhuman authority behind it."

—*Albert Einstein,*
Albert Einstein, the Human Side:
New Glimpses from His Archives

Ethics is the system of values that governs behavior. To inquire whether a particular action is ethical is to ask if it aligns with the right values. Sometimes the term "ethics" is contrasted with "morality," in an attempt to draw a distinction between the "ethical" as that which is good versus the "moral" as that which is socially accepted or within social mores. Much of the time, however, these terms are used interchangeably. The question of which ethical values should guide our lives and what actions are ethical is controversial and without consensus on most issues.

There are many reasons for the controversy surrounding ethics. Two of the main reasons that there is wide disagreement about ethical principles and ethical answers on specific issues are: 1) there is little agreement on the authoritative source of ethical values, and 2) even with agreement on a source of ethical values, there is still wide disagreement about what these values are and how they apply to real-life ethical dilemmas.

Religion has a long history of providing guidance on ethics and, even today, continues to be the source of ethical authority for many people—if not most—around the world. Of course, there are numerous religions with different, and often conflicting, ethical values. Many Jewish and Islamic people consider eating pork to be forbidden by their religion, whereas most Christians do not have such a taboo. Certain religions believe in polygamous marriage; in Islam, polygyny, or the practice of having multiple wives, is allowed and a man may have up to four wives. Modern Christianity generally rejects this practice, although the Mormon Church in the United States did not renounce the practice of polygyny until 1890. Same-sex marriage is considered a sin in the Roman Catholic Church and the United Methodist Church, but is accepted by the Episcopal Church and the United Church of Christ. Therefore, even if religion is the source of ethics, this will not resolve the wide disagreement about particular societal issues.

Nonreligious, or secular, individuals often live by particular value systems and claim that religion is not needed for ethics. Many nonreligious and religious people have embraced an ethical system known as humanism, which holds that ethical values come from rational discovery and are established by human nature. Rather than seeing ethics as something established by a god or the gods of a certain religion, secular ethics sees morality rooted in facts about humanity. A secular ethical system may hold that ethical values are discovered by rational thought or are established by certain details about human beings, such as the ability to feel pain or the desire for freedom. As with religious ethical systems, however, there is no one secular ethical system that has all the same answers on ethical principles and specific ethical issues.

The question of what is ethical—what is right and wrong, good and evil, virtuous and vicious—has been debated for thousands of years. The Greek philosophers posited a notion of the ethical person with an emphasis on developing a virtuous character through learning and practice. In the Middle Ages, philosophers such as Thomas Aquinas discussed ethics as an outgrowth of Christian theology. During the Age of Enlightenment, German philosopher Immanuel Kant developed a theory of ethics based on reason, ushering in a new era of ethics as a practice distinct from, although compatible with, religion. In the nineteenth century, British philosophers Jeremy Bentham and John Stuart Mill changed the face of ethics by positing utilitarianism, an ethical theory that roots ethical decisions in the principle of utility, thus making ethical decisions into empirical issues of maximizing pleasure or happiness. Modern philosophers of ethics draw from all of these traditions.

Certain ethical issues are not controversial at first glance. Almost no one argues against the claim that unprovoked killing of an innocent fellow human being is wrong. However, the basis for believing this is varied. Is it because human life is sacred? Is it because it violates one of the Ten Commandments? Is it because we should not cause pain through our actions? Although resolving these questions might not make much of a difference to the answer in this particular situation, it makes quite a bit of difference when looking at other ethical issues. In *Opposing Viewpoints: Ethics*, authors take a variety of viewpoints on the subject of ethics in chapters titled "What Is the Basis for Ethics?," "What Ethics Should Guide Decisions About Life?," "Should Religious Beliefs About Ethics Justify Behavior?," and "How Should Ethics Guide Economic Policies?" The divergent viewpoints in this volume illustrate that there is wide disagreement about sources of ethics and the principles for reaching answers to specific ethical dilemmas.

OPPOSING
VIEWPOINTS®
SERIES

CHAPTER 1

What Is the Basis for Ethics?

Chapter Preface

A 2014 survey by the Pew Research Center's Global Attitudes Project found that many people around the world believe that it is necessary to believe in God to be a moral person. For many people, the basis for ethics is in religion, and they believe that without religion, a person will not have the right ethical guidance.

In the United States, an increasing number of adults identify as unaffiliated with religion. The latest Religious Landscape Survey by the Pew Religion and Public Life Project, conducted in 2007, found that more than 16 percent of Americans are unaffiliated with any religion. For these Americans at the least, any ethical beliefs would not come from religion or God.

Pew found that the viewpoint that it is necessary to believe in God to be moral is more prominent in Latin America, Asia, and Africa, and less prominent in Europe and North America. However, the United States was the only country among European and North American nations surveyed where a majority of people stated that it is necessary to believe in God to be moral: 53 percent said they believed this, whereas 46 percent said it is not necessary to believe in God to be moral. In Pakistan, Indonesia, and Ghana, more than 95 percent of people said one must believe in God to be moral. In Spain, the Czech Republic, France, and China, less than 20 percent of people believe this is so.

In the United States, a majority of Americans are concerned about the moral and ethical climate. A 2014 Gallup poll found that only 5 percent are very satisfied with the moral and ethical climate in the United States. Thirty percent each were somewhat satisfied and somewhat dissatisfied, but almost a third—32 percent—were very dissatisfied with the moral and ethical climate. The dissatisfaction may in part be due to the wide disagreement about the basis for ethics and the ensuing disagreement about the answers to pressing moral issues.

As the viewpoints in this chapter illustrate, the idea that religion is necessary for ethics is far from established, and the source of ethical authority continues to be debated. Several authors note that there is a renewed interest in ethics of late, particularly in the secular realm, outside of any organized religion.

"*The idea that something might be spiritually harmful (or beneficial) in a way that can't be demonstrated statistically has been written out of the conversation.*"

Moral Relativism, R.I.P.

Helen Rittelmeyer

In the following viewpoint, Helen Rittelmeyer argues that moral relativism—the idea that there are no moral absolute truths, but only those true for individuals or certain groups—is no longer a cultural threat. She claims that the new threat is an understanding of ethical controversies as essentially questions to be answered by science, which denies that some acts may be harmful or beneficial in a way that cannot be quantified. Rittelmeyer is a policy analyst in the Social Foundations Program at the Centre for Independent Studies in Sydney, Australia.

As you read, consider the following questions:

1. Rittelmeyer claims that there are traces of relativism in what four principles?

2. The author claims that the top dangerous amoralism is no longer relativism but what theory?

Helen Rittelmeyer, "Moral Relativism, R.I.P.," *American Spectator*, vol. 45, no. 7, September 2012, p. 40. Copyright © 2012 by The American Spectator. All rights reserved. Reproduced by permission.

3. Rittelmeyer contends that conservatives should be happy that Americans are now wanting moral claims of what sort?

Any conservative who expends energy denouncing relativism is wasting his time fighting the last war. Relativism was quite a force for evil in its day, but the vitality has gone out of it. The villain that once needed an army of culture warriors to fight it back now requires, at most, one armed guard by its hospital bed to keep the decrepit thing from escaping. Someone like David Horowitz or Roger Kimball could do the job single-handedly.

But it will not be easy for the Right to declare victory and move on. Moral relativism has become the culture-war equivalent of racketeering—no indictment is complete without it. Relativism has been blamed for the financial crisis, Obamacare, and Kanye West. When Michele Bachmann admitted earlier this year that she and her husband were dual Swiss-American citizens, a *National Review* blogger called it a "testament to how thoroughly the moral relativism of the postnational left has permeated our culture." Even Rep. Paul Ryan, who is no Rick Santorum, told an interviewer last year, "If you ask me what the biggest problem in America is, I'm not going to tell you debt, deficits, statistics, economics—I'll tell you it's moral relativism."

Relativism has become such a routine charge that half the people who invoke it feel no need to do more than gesture toward the culture at large by way of explanation. But we've come a long way since the days when Marilyn Manson and Andres Serrano (the artist behind *Piss Christ*) could make careers out of transgression for transgression's sake. Breaking taboos for shock value is relativism; breaking taboos as a means rather than an end is not, which gives Lady Gaga and Seth MacFarlane an alibi. Pop stars used to think that authenticity was an important part of a musician's job description—that's what those Lilith Fair songstresses, self-righteous grungers, and way-too-honest emo kids seemed to think, anyway—and it certainly was a form of relativism to make such a fetish of being true to yourself, objective standards be damned. But overprocessed chart-slayers like Katy Perry and Ke$ha don't act as if they want to be judged by the brutal honesty of their self-expression, and neither do mannered indie darlings like the Decemberists. As for cinema, anti-heroes are out and heroes are back in. Virtue, authority, and law and order are all in fashion, as the bank accounts of Chris Nolan, J.K. Rowling, and Marvel Comics will attest. There are still plenty of enemies for conservative culture warriors to fight, but relativism is no longer one of them.

Not that the Right's overreliance on relativism as a term of abuse was justified to begin with. There are traces of relativism in pluralism, freedom of speech, cosmopolitanism, foreign-policy realism, and a thousand other principles, including many that conservatives like. With the help of good judgment, these concepts have allowed the West to find a middle ground between nihilism and absolutism. Promiscuous use of the R word only makes that project more difficult. It is also—and this is a personal opinion—mind-numbingly dull. "Some things are good, others are bad," has sometimes been an extremely important point to make, but never has it been an interesting one.

A cynic might say that accusations of relativism are so popular because they are just as evasive as relativism itself, and they end conversations just as abruptly. If relativism is an easy way to avoid saying why something is bad, calling your opponent a relativist is a way to escape explaining why your own opinion is good. It stacks the deck in the accuser's favor: He doesn't need a compelling position to win the argument; just having a position will do. Even when the Right's opponents really were relativists, this looked like a lazy defense.

Readers who are skeptical that relativism is moribund should realize, first of all, that it seems much more influential than it really is. Those of its adherents who got jobs in our various cultural establishments over the last couple of decades are still there, only now they have seniority or, worse, tenure. But behind that veneer of power, relativism is doing no better than communism was in Eastern Europe in the 1990s. After the Iron Curtain fell, the Polish and Czech bureaucracies were still staffed by the same apparatchiks as before, but only because no one, not even Lech Walesa, can conjure an experienced workforce out of thin air. The party itself was mostly defunct, its ideology even more so. The countries of Eastern Europe, like the last redoubts of relativism in the U.S., will find new ways to fail, but they won't fail in that particular way again.

The decline of relativism is difficult to explain because—again, like communism—it's not clear whether conservative opponents, liberal reformers, or flaws inherent in the system itself were ultimately responsible for its downfall. But, with the benefit of hindsight, the basic outline of relativism's rise and fall has become clear enough. As well as revealing a lesson or two, this story might indicate which mind-set has taken relativism's place as the most serious internal threat to Western culture. I suspect I know where the danger now lies, and if I've guessed correctly, then carrying on about relativism will have the perverse effect of strengthening the enemy that the Right should be trying to weaken.

BUT FIRST THINGS FIRST. The war against relativism, like many of us, had its finest days back in college. The rhetoric was grandiose, and the players behaved theatrically: Allan Bloom and his allies indulged their histrionic sides almost as much as the teenagers did. Everyone in America who had ever attended college felt qualified to join in the fight, which turned an academic dispute into a nationwide brawl. It was serious business, but it was also a lot of fun.

The Closing of the American Mind had its 25th anniversary this year, and a number of people marked the event by publishing tributes to the book's continuing relevance. I am reluctant to consign any good crotchet to the dustbin, especially one of such erudition and grumpiness, but the war Allan Bloom launched is all over bar the shouting. Relativists are an endangered species on America's campuses, and in 30 years they will probably be extinct—or, if not, then sequestered in made-up departments that are denigrated by the rest of the faculty and eyed predatorily by budget directors on the lookout for programs to cut.

The Yale English Department is a good example. In the directory for tenured and tenure-track faculty, "Marxist literary theory" is listed by five professors among their fields of interest, "gender and sexuality" by nine, and "colonial and postcolonial" by 11, or a quarter of the 44 professors. In the graduate student directory, however, the numbers for those subjects are one, three, and a fat goose egg. That's quite a statistical drop-off, considering that grad students outnumber professors nearly two to one. The topics favored instead by these future scholars are Romanticism (six), Victorian literature (five), Milton (seven), and, oddly enough, religious literature (also seven). Honorable mentions include "Biblical exegesis," "conversion narratives," and "Middle English devotional, visionary, and anchoritic writing"—they're not just reading the Bible, they're reading monks.

The next generation of college professors seems to have returned to the proper business of contemplating the best that has been thought and said in the world (admittedly with some progressive politics thrown in). Why this reversal? One possibility is that academics saw some merit in the blasts against postmodern celebrities. Another possibility is that everyone simply got bored. It can be mentally stimulating to come up with arguments for dumb positions like "*Madame Bovary* is in no way superior to *I, Rigoberta Menchu*" or "Everyone in *Hamlet* is secretly homosexual," but these arguments are like noodly jazz: fun to play, dreadful to listen to.

I also suspect that professors who embraced relativism when it seemed rebellious and exciting got spooked when they met the first batch of students who had grown up on the postmodern cant they'd been spouting—kids who wanted to study literature not because they loved books, but because they saw in relativism an excellent playground for their own vanity. The same thing happens when libertarians have children. They sober up fast once they realize that, in an immature creature with no self-restraint to fall back on, antinomianism is a terrifying thing.

On the subject of antinomianism and kids too young to handle it, one of relativism's most pernicious bequests was the self-esteem fad in K–12 public schools, which declared "being yourself" the summum bonum of education. This manifestation of relativism will probably still be clinging to life when all the others have vanished, thanks to public education's sclerotic bureaucracy and behemoth teachers' unions. However, that stranglehold is being threatened by charter schools—and it's very revealing to note which kind of charter is threatening it most. Highly regimented inner-city schools like Chicago's Noble Charter Network or the KIPP system have captured the imagination of large chunks of the Left (including some of the same people who, five years ago, condemned charter schools as privatization by stealth). These schools have longer hours, make students wear coat-and-tie uniforms, and above all, preach discipline. Noble fines pupils $5 for failing to make eye contact with a teacher or for missing buttons on their school uniforms. It also has a strong record of success, with more than 80 percent of graduates entering college, most of them the first in their families to do so. The entrenched relativists may end up winning the political battle and robbing charters of their government subsidies, but that's a political question. The cultural question has already been settled, and the relativists haven't just lost, they've driven the public to embrace the opposite extreme.

The Underpinnings of Moral Thought

Over the last three centuries . . . the Judeo-Christian underpinnings of Western culture have been shaken, eroded, and ultimately rejected altogether by new, man-centered ways of viewing reality. The rise of science and the unrivaled hegemony of the scientific method—advancements that undeniably increase technological and material comforts for countless billions of human beings—also destroyed the very premises on which moral truth and consensus had been constructed. Faith no longer carried any weight in a world that sought truth only in data that could be verified empirically. Scripture became reduced to mere mythology in the face of our implacable march toward the conquest of nature, the only realm available to the study of physics and biology, based as they are on sensory observation and perception. And as theology became synonymous with superstition, and faith in God the intellectual parallel of believing in unicorns and leprechauns, the transcendent foundation of Western morality—that which kept it all together, anchored in a better world than this, and supported by a mind much greater than ours—vanished into thin air.

Duke Pesta,
"Moral Relativism and the Crisis of Contemporary Education,"
New American, *December 5, 2011.*

Almost everywhere outside the galleries of Chelsea and the hole-in-the-wall theatres of off-Broadway, relativism is a spent force. That's what makes it so frustrating to watch young conservatives waste time inveighing against an enemy that the previous generation has already knocked out, or at least sent to the canvass—especially when there are more threatening trends that need refuting. My own nominee for the top spot in the dangerous-amoralism stakes is utilitarianism, which America's secularized elite has taken to new extremes. Relativism claimed that we could sidestep moral controversies by letting everyone decide ethical questions for themselves; the new utilitarianism claims that there are no moral controversies, just empirical ones. Technocratic optimism has always been part of the Left's political philosophy. What's new is its influence on culture.

In the last culture war, relativism's influence was evident in the stock arguments that kept appearing in magazines and op-ed pages: breaking taboos is valuable for its own sake; people have a right to make their own choices and not be judged for it; what you call a social evil is really just a cultural difference; et cetera. But those articles are no longer seen so often. Now, the most annoyingly ubiquitous genre in journalism is the social-scientific analysis, as if a person can't speak with authority without citing economics or sociology. This is bad enough in political conversation, but it has begun to affect people's ethical thinking. Under the new cultural rules, moral condemnation is a legitimate thing to express, but only if you can demonstrate that the sin you want to condemn makes someone twice as likely to take antidepressants or 40 percent less likely to be promoted at work. Malcolm Gladwell and the *Freakonomics* guys have more moral authority than the archbishop of New York. Great artists are producing movies, TV shows, and songs about tough moral dilemmas, but although liberals buy the tickets and the albums, they don't take the art they consume very seriously. When moral questions arise, they forget *The Wire* and the Hold Steady and ask what the studies show.

An excellently ludicrous example of this mind-set was offered by an article on weight loss I read earlier this summer. It opened by citing a handful of studies showing obesity to be correlated not just with heart disease but also with slower career advancement and a greater likelihood of developing mental-health problems. Let's leave aside the fact that the author didn't feel he could take the undesirability of being fat as a given. The bigger problem is that this sort of argument tries to have it both ways—to have all the benefits of authority without the burden of being answerable to people who disagree. On one hand, the author isn't saying obesity is bad, science is, which makes it a fact and not an opinion. Your personal experience or common sense might tell you that a few extra pounds aren't always such a disaster; but that just means you're in the statistical minority for whom these bad outcomes do not eventuate. In other words: My moral claim is objectively correct, but that doesn't mean it has to be true in your case. The same evasive maneuver can be seen in the argument that there's nothing wrong with pornography because its prevalence isn't correlated with higher crime rates, or that there's nothing wrong with gay marriage as long as children of same-sex couples aren't more likely to receive reduced-price lunches at school. The idea that something might be spiritually harmful (or beneficial) in a way that can't be demonstrated statistically has been written out of the conversation.

The columnist Theodore Dalrymple believes that this new form of moral abdication, like the last one, was born on college campuses:

> The vast expansion of tertiary education has increased by orders of magnitude the numbers of people who think in sociological abstractions rather than in concrete moral terms. Statistical generalizations are more real to them, and certainly more important, than the trifling moral dilemmas of their own lives.

Now that Shakespeare is out of the dead-white-guy doghouse, perhaps colleges could reverse some of the damage they've done by teaching *All's Well That Ends Well*, which opens with Parolles trying to convince Helena to change her attitude toward sexual continence:

> Loss of virginity is rational increase, and there was never
> virgin got till virginity was first lost. That you were made of
> is metal to make virgins. Virginity by being once lost may be
> ten times found; by being ever kept, it is ever lost.

The idea that promiscuity would yield a net increase in
virginity makes perfect sense quantitatively but no sense morally. It's just the sort of thing an economist could prove. It is
also self-evidently ridiculous, even to a person accustomed to
treating moral questions technocratically.

The great attraction of this new utilitarian mind-set is its
certainty—the fact that answers to such questions are not just
a matter of opinion (and therefore, not relative)—which is
why continuing to demonize the old enemy only makes the
new one more appealing. Conservatives should be pleased,
maybe even a little proud, that Americans are in the market
for moral claims they can make with authority, but now it's
time to worry about which authorities they choose to trust.
Economics can tell a country how to satisfy its desires effi-
ciently, but not which desires are noble. Sociologists can put
out a survey asking whether people are happy or fulfilled, but
can't give them the moral vocabulary they need to make sense
of the difference between happiness and mere contentment, or
between fulfillment and shallow self-regard. Some social-
scientific studies make claims that turn out to be false, and
others make claims that are correct on their own terms but
not in the messy world of the human soul. The culture war
goes on, and probably always will, but constant condemnation
of relativism has become a distraction. As long as technocratic
amorality keeps trying to turn every cultural question into a
matter of optimization, the Right can't afford any distractions.

*"Traditional religious people are in the
way, and many of our fellow Americans are doing their best to push us out
of the way."*

With Religion on the Decline,
Secular Values Are on the Rise

R.R. Reno

*In the following viewpoint, R.R. Reno argues that religious free-
dom in the United States has changed drastically in the last two
centuries, shifting from the freedom to practice religion to the
freedom to be free from religion. Reno contends that this rise in
anti-religion among the elite is leading to trends in the law and
in values that are at odds with the traditional morals of religious
people. Reno is the editor of* First Things *magazine.*

As you read, consider the following questions:

1. According to Reno, which amendment to the US Constitution protects religious freedom?

2. What fraction of the US population currently checks
   "none" when asked about religious affiliation, according
   to the author?

3. For the past fifty years, approximately what percentage of the population in the United States has attended church every Sunday, according to Reno?

Americans are rightly proud of our tradition of religious liberty. The founders recognized that religious convictions cut very deeply into the soul, making people capable of great sacrifices—and often stimulating bitter conflicts and terrible persecutions. Thus, we have the First Amendment and its definition of the first freedom: "Congress shall make no law respecting an establishment of religion, or prohibiting the free exercise thereof."

We need to recognize, however, that our approach to religious freedom has in fact changed a great deal in the more than 200 years of national history. These changes reflect shifts in the overarching religious consensus in the United States. By my reading of the signs of the times, this consensus is changing yet again. The shift foretells a renegotiation and redefinition of the nature and scope of religious liberty—one that I fear will not favor religious believers.

The Three Phases of Religious Liberty

There have been three main phases or agreements about religious liberty in our country. The first was a federalism that recognized local forms of establishment but wished to keep the national government out of the religion business. The second corresponded to the long century of ecumenical Protestant hegemony that naturally intertwined itself with state power. And the third, which followed the Second World War, has been characterized by a move toward religious neutrality.

Phase One. At the time the Constitution was written, the Congregational Church was established in Massachusetts and Connecticut, and it received public support from tax revenue. In Georgia and South Carolina, the Anglican or Episcopal Church was established. It was not until *Everson v. Board of*

Education in 1947 that the Supreme Court stipulated that non-establishment and free exercise applied to the states as well as the federal government. Nevertheless, soon after the nation was founded, elite opinion consolidated around a view that government should remain at a distance from religion. This consensus had two sources: one focused on the rights of individual conscience and the other on the integrity of the church as an independent institution.

This position led to disestablishment in the states, culminating with Massachusetts in 1830. It is important to recognize, however, that this consensus was very pro-religion. Political and cultural leaders did not want any particular denomination to have privileged access to state power, but they were in favor of a religious society and thus a religiously inspired public culture. Or, to be more accurate, they were in favor of a Protestant society and a Protestant-inspired government.

Phase Two. By the time of crusading abolitionism and the formation of the Republican Party in 1854, the ascendancy of a pan-Protestant consensus was in full swing. It reached its high point with Prohibition. A person can still find public monuments in many American cities dedicated to the crusade against demon rum. They often feature an expanded list of theological virtues: faith, hope, love—and temperance. The insertion of "under God" into the Pledge of Allegiance in 1954 was a late, defensive expression of the power of this consensus, which was already being challenged by a new secularism.

The Protestant consensus encouraged anti-Catholicism in culture as well as law. In 1875 President Ulysses S. Grant urged the creation of public schools "unmixed with sectarian, pagan or atheistical dogmas." Nonsectarian and non-atheistical meant schools that could be trusted to inculcate American values, meaning generic and non-dogmatic Protestant values, which were considered the finest expression of true freedom. Here religious freedom means the freedom to be a generic

Protestant, with Catholicism grudgingly tolerated at best, and Mormons subject to intense persecution. The courts interpreted religious freedom accordingly.

The Protestant consensus became more capacious as the 20th century wore on. After World War II it expanded to include Judaism and Catholicism, and we came to think of ourselves as a religious nation committed to Judeo-Christian values. But as the religious consensus expanded, it also eroded. Influential writers like H.L. Mencken mocked religious believers, reflecting an increasingly confident and outspoken view that religion—especially traditional Christianity—is a social liability that hinders progress. Many factors contributed to this emerging opinion. The abject failure of Prohibition soured many on Protestantism's crusading spirit. Newly emerging Protestant fundamentalism was self-consciously antagonistic and reflected an anti-establishment populism. For many the threat to society changed. Whatever their personal beliefs, the founders thought religion good for society and atheism a threat. By contrast, for someone like Mr. Mencken or Clarence Darrow or Margaret Sanger, religion was the problem.

Phase Three. Our constitutional interpretation came to reflect this new development. It shifted toward an ideal of religious neutrality. The Supreme Court decision in 1947 that applied the prohibition of religious establishment to the states led to the development of a complex set of legal rules limiting the role of religion in public life.

Law professors rightly seek to clarify this jurisprudence, but for our purposes I think a broad but largely accurate simplification will suffice: Our constitutional law concerning religious liberty sought to secure an orderly separation of religion from the social influence the Protestant era had encouraged. This separation has helped protect small religious minorities from undue public control, but the major emphasis has been on restraining the influence of religious majorities.

Preoccupations with prayer at high school graduation ceremonies provide the most obvious example. The court has been eager to protect the tender conscience of the lonely, unbelieving student from the supposedly great social pressures of an anodyne interdenominational prayer by a local pastor. The danger is not that a hard-line Calvinist will impose his doctrines on wishy-washy Methodists, which the founders worried about. Instead, the court after World War II reflected a broader concern that believers of all stripes are too predominant and therefore make unbelievers feel uncomfortable and excluded. Freedom *of* religion therefore means the option of being free *from* religion. I believe this emphasis will characterize the next phase of our history: the shift from individual freedom from religion to a vision of society as a whole free from religious influence.

The Anti-Religious Cohort

Over the last few decades the Mencken cohort has grown. In the 1950s around 3 percent of Americans checked the "none" box in surveys asking about religious affiliation. Now 20 percent of the population does so. Moreover, these so-called "nones" are heavily represented in elite culture. A recent report on family life from the University of Virginia's Institute for Advanced Studies in Culture identifies parents they call the "engaged progressives." Representing 21 percent of parents, this group is the most highly educated and most influential. It overlaps with the nones. Fewer than 20 percent in this group go to church regularly. More than half never attend.

In itself, this demographic change need not foretell dramatic changes in law. A significant segment of Americans who do not go to church might support the now established postwar trend toward religious neutrality: the belief that the country needs to make space for unbelievers and not presume their adherence to a religious consensus, however vague. But the nones and engaged progressives are not just irreligious. They are often anti-religious and eager to limit the influence of traditional Christianity.

As the study observes, engaged progressive parents value tolerance and diversity, but their overall moral outlook puts them at odds with many religious people. Nones and engaged progressives overwhelming support abortion and gay marriage, for example. They are also highly partisan; an overwhelming majority vote for liberal candidates and have thus become a key pillar of the Democratic Party. This moral and political profile makes them hostile to traditional religion. The study explains: "The only type of diversity that engaged progressives might tacitly oppose within their children's friendship network would be a born-again Christian."

The anti-religious instinct of this cohort came into the open during the last election cycle. Delegates to the Democratic National Convention notoriously struck the word *God* from the party platform, only to have it halfheartedly restored by anxious party leaders. During the election, the talking points included attacking the Republican "war on women." This well-crafted slogan was designed to rally the nones, the secular base that is now the largest identifiable constituency in the Democratic Party.

Institutions of cultural authority tell us what is good and respectable—and what is bad and shameful. It is now crushingly obvious that this machinery, which can include museums, universities, foundations or mainstream media, reflects many of the values of the nones and engaged progressives. From their point of view, traditional Christianity is quaint when confined to exotic liturgies or remote Amish communities, but it most certainly should not influence the future of American culture and politics.

This shift toward antagonism cannot help but affect our attitudes toward religious liberty. Our Constitution accords rights to the people, and the courts cannot void them willy-

---

The Influence of Religion

At the present time, do you think religion as a whole is increasing its influence on American life or losing its influence?

Church Attendance	Increasing Its Influence %	Losing Its Influence %
Weekly	20	77
Nearly weekly/monthly	25	72
Less often	18	79

TAKEN FROM: Gallup poll, May 2–7, 2013.

---

nilly. Therefore, unless the Constitution is amended, there will always be a prohibition of establishment and a right of free exercise. But history shows that the Constitution is a plastic document. When elite culture thinks something is bad for society as a whole, judges find ways to suppress it. In the late 19th century, for example, the First Amendment offered no protection for Mormons. In 1890 the Supreme Court upheld the Edmunds-Tucker Act of 1887, legislation that prohibited polygamy and dissolved the Church of Jesus Christ of Latter-day Saints and confiscated its property.

Trends in Jurisprudence

Not surprisingly, law professors today who view traditional Christianity as a social threat are beginning to theorize changes to the law. I see three trends. The first and most obvious involves what I have called the Selma analogy: the equation of gay liberation with the historic struggle for civil rights for black Americans. The second shifts from freedom of religion to freedom of worship. The third hopes to redefine religious liberty as a general liberty of conscience.

The civil rights laws adopted in the 1960s were designed to bulldoze racism out of American public life, and the Selma analogy prepares the way for a narrowing of religious freedom by equating dissent from progressive values with discrimination. Proponents of gay rights, for example, believe the freedom of religious individuals and institutions should be limited if they do not conform to the new consensus about sexual morality.

Some judges already agree. In 2008 the New Mexico Human Rights Commission determined that wedding photographers violated the state's antidiscrimination law by refusing to photograph a lesbian commitment ceremony. The photographers, Elaine and Jonathan Huguenin, appealed to the New Mexico Supreme Court, arguing that their religious views about marriage prevented them from photographing the ceremony. The court was not sympathetic. It applied what is called the "public accommodation doctrine" of civil rights law: those offering services to the general public may not discriminate. This doctrine overrides a great deal of what we think of as religious liberty.

In a concurring opinion Justice Richard C. Bosson put it clearly: "The Huguenins are free to think, to say, to believe, as they wish; they may pray to the God of their choice and follow those commandments in their personal lives wherever they lead," but "in the smaller, more focused world of the marketplace, of commerce, of public accommodation," they have to abide by antidiscrimination laws. This is "the price of citizenship," he wrote. Apparently this price includes the violation of religious conscience when it comes to gay rights, which makes it seem that religious freedom is only allowed in the privacy of home or the precincts of church.

The shift toward a private, personal freedom that lacks space for public expression has become prominent in the ways the [Barack] Obama administration talks about religious freedom. The International Religious Freedom Act of 1998 sought to make religious freedom a diplomatic priority. The current administration consistently reframes this priority as freedom of worship. The shift in language is understandable. The United States has many allies in the Muslim world for whom anything like our approach to religious liberty is at best a remote possibility. For different reasons the same is the case in China and elsewhere. The danger, however, is that this narrow understanding of religious freedom will gain traction in our domestic debates and become another way for legal theorists to argue for a minimal interpretation of the First Amendment.

The Selma analogy and the diminution of religious liberty to a bare freedom of worship represent two ways to redefine the First Amendment. Added to these, I see a third and more dramatic threat: today some law professors ask why religious people should get special rights in the first place. Why should a Catholic or a Baptist or a Hindu get special constitutional protection, but not a committed utilitarian or ardent socialist? Evoking the principle of fairness, some now argue that the conscience of every person needs legal protection, not just consciences formed by religious traditions. Thus, the First Amendment needs to be reinterpreted to provide freedom of conscience, not freedom of religion.

This mentality is libertarian and is gaining traction, not the least because it seems to expand rather than limit freedom. (Even representatives of the church can sometimes seem to imply this when they focus on conscience.) But the promise of expansion is an illusion. Libertarianism theorizes an unworkable system: If the conscience of every person must be equally respected, then we will have freedom of conscience only when nothing important is at stake.

There is no guarantee that our legal culture will follow the trajectories I have outlined. Judges are influenced by good legal arguments, and the defenders of religious freedom today may succeed in breaking down the Selma analogy and reverse the trend to attenuate religious freedom by redefining it as freedom of worship. The current membership of the U.S. Supreme Court has shown itself very firmly aligned with a robust approach to religious freedom. There are reasons to be hopeful in the near term. But history shows that the rule of law generally reflects what the social consensus believes is conducive to the common good. The law ministers to culture, not the other way around. The nones and other progressives are frustrated by the influence of traditional Christianity over American society. This makes me pessimistic about the medium and long term.

The Heart of the Conflict

To be blunt: Religious people who hold traditional values are in the way of what many powerful people want. We are in the way of widespread acceptance of abortion, unrestricted embryonic stem cell research and experimentation with fetal tissue. We are in the way of doctor-assisted suicide, euthanasia and the mercy killing of genetically defective infants. We are in the way of new reproductive technologies, which will become more important as our society makes sex more sterile. We are in the way of gay rights and the redefinition of marriage. We are in the way of the nones and the engaged progressives and their larger goal of deconstructing traditional moral limits so that they can be reconstructed in accord with their vision of the future.

Traditional religious people are in the way, and many of our fellow Americans are doing their best to push us out of the way. The outspoken among us have been largely expelled from higher education and other institutions of cultural authority. This exclusion should not surprise us. Traditional Christianity and churchgoing no longer define the social consensus in the United States. The Protestant era is over, and in its demise we have not seen the Catholic moment that the Rev. Richard John Neuhaus, founder of *First Things*, hoped for. Instead, we seem to be heading into the secular moment, which is almost certain to find ways to redefine religious liberty, or at least try.

In Islamic states, a *dhimmi* is a non-Muslim who is tolerated, but whose social existence is carefully circumscribed to ensure no threat to Muslim dominance. Have we reached the point at which our secular elites envision something similar for religious people with traditional values? We will be free to worship, but not to run universities or hospitals or social service agencies in accord with our principles. We will be free to believe as we wish, but not to run our businesses in accord with our beliefs. We will be permitted to exist, as long as we do not openly challenge the progressive consensus.

Religious people need to support the good legal minds fighting for our freedom, but it is even more important that we fight against the temptation to accept *dhimmitude*. Yes, antagonism toward traditional Christianity is now common in our ruling class. One prejudice warmly approved by many secularists is that against so-called fundamentalists. But we need to remember that the secular moment does not correspond to religious decline. The committed core of believers, defined as those who attend church every Sunday, has remained remarkably constant for the last 50 years at between 25 to 35 percent of the population in the United States. Furthermore, the secular moment has no grassroots legacy to compare with the scope and commitment of the pro-life and homeschooling movements.

It is appropriate to conclude, therefore, with words of encouragement. Last summer, a young Dominican brother studying for the priesthood served as an intern for *First Things*. He is an impressive man, one of a remarkable cohort of 20 who entered the Dominican Friars of the Province of St. Joseph a few years ago to begin formation. As I walked with him on the streets of New York City, I noticed that people often stare at his white, ankle-length outfit. Unlike the often-wild fashion statements that people parade as great expressions of protest or individuality but blend into the city as just another pose or posture, his simple habit represents something dangerously real. People intuit, however dimly, that he embodies a vision of the future that collides with the spirit of our age, and does so with frightening force.

Seeing these reactions, I was reminded that our faith goes deep, very deep. And as the guardian and servant of this faith, the church has tremendous power. As I contemplate the coming battles over religious freedom, I am consoled by this thought: Our secular challengers are right, very right, to see our faith as a dangerous and disruptive dissent.

*"The needs these congregations aim to
fulfill aren't religious, but human."*

Secular Congregations Promote Humanist Values and Morals

Adam Lee

*In the following viewpoint, Adam Lee argues that the growth of
atheist and secular communities is a positive development for
the growing number of Americans that do not identify with religion. Lee contends that these so-called atheist churches provide a
forum for members to share humanist ethics, support each other,
and build community without the requirement of belief in a
particular religion but with shared humanist values. Lee is the
author of* Daylight Atheism *and writes a blog of the same name.*

As you read, consider the following questions:

1. Approximately how many million members of the millennial generation have no religion, according to Lee?

2. Lee claims that almost all so-called atheist churches in-
   corporate ethics in what way?

3. According to the author, atheist communities create a positive image to counter negative stereotypes about atheists such as what?

In the last 30 years, atheism and secularism have been booming in America. As many as one in four members of the millennial generation now say they have no religion. Given the vast size of the millennials—78 million people, slightly more than the baby boomers—that adds up to almost 20 million freethinking Americans. And from all indications, the up-and-coming generations are even more secular.

The Atheist Community

As the broader atheist community becomes larger and better organized, secularists and freethinkers have shown increasing interest in gathering together with like-minded people. Atheist community isn't a brand-new phenomenon; there have long been local meet-ups as well as regional and national conventions, like Skepticon, the giant free conference that takes place every year in Springfield, Missouri, or the Reason Rally, the nationwide gathering of atheists and humanists on the National Mall in March 2012. But many of these conferences are focused on activism and political mobilization, and as necessary as those are, they don't appeal to everyone.

That's why, in just the last few months and years, we're witnessing a new wave of secular communities—atheist churches, if you insist—whose focus is on doing good, living well and appreciating the wonder and beauty of the world without recourse to archaic mythology.

The most prominent of these is the Sunday Assembly. Founded in north London in January 2013 by two stand-up comedians, Pippa Evans and Sanderson Jones, the Sunday Assembly is a godless congregation—all the best parts of church but without the religion, in the words of its founders, whose motto is "Live better. Help often. Wonder more." It was almost immediately a rousing success, attracting hundreds of people, and has spread to other British cities, including Brighton, Bristol and Oxford.

But the Sunday Assembly has much larger ambitions. Its founders helped organize services in New York City [NYC] over the summer, and recently launched an American "40 Dates and 40 Nights" tour, barnstorming across the country to hold well-attended services in Boston, Washington, D.C., San Jose, San Diego, Los Angeles, and more (even Nashville!), aiming to drum up support for U.S. satellite congregations. Sunday Assembly meetings have also been held in Australia, including in Sydney, Adelaide and Melbourne.

The Humanist Movement

Though it's attracted the most media attention, the Sunday Assembly isn't the only atheist gathering emerging from this crystallizing secular community. In Houston, Texas, ex-pastor-turned-atheist Mike Aus founded the Houston Oasis, "a community grounded in reason, celebrating the human experience." Its Sunday gatherings host live music from local bands, secular humanist-themed sermons, and community service projects, like blood donation drives. Mesa, Arizona, now has a humanist community center, thanks to the Humanist Society of Greater Phoenix, and the Humanist Community of Harvard offers a nontheistic support network for students.

In Canada, there's the Calgary Secular Church, founded by Korey Peters and another local activist. It meets twice a month: once for casual conversation, once for a more structured service that incorporates a humanist liturgy and a presentation from a rotating slate of speakers, on topics like children's rights versus parents' rights, abortion, free will, or even the existence of intelligent alien life. The Sunday meetings include free child care and a potluck brunch. As Peters says, "For some, our meetings are the only place they are allowed to say they have no faith, and that has proved quite valuable. We provide community as well, so these people now are building fellow non-religious friendships . . . our main value for atheists is that we are making a world that is safe for them to live in."

Not all of these efforts are brand new. For instance, there's Ethical Culture, a humanist movement founded in the 1870s by the reformer Felix Adler, focusing on "deeds, not creeds." Ethical Culture societies still exist today, most concentrated in the New York metropolitan area (including its flagship location in Manhattan), but it can be found in other large cities across the U.S. like Austin, Baltimore, Boston, St. Louis, Philadelphia and Washington, D.C.

There's also Unitarian Universalism [UU], a nontheistic religion that arose in 1961 from the merger of unitarianism and universalism, two liberal Christian denominations. But it's evolved beyond its Christian origins to become a truly creedless church. It has no official dogma or statement of faith, just seven foundational principles which relate to moral living, not belief. Surveys suggest that a plurality of UUs are atheists (although it must be said that the Unitarian Universalist Association also has at least a few highly placed anti-atheist bigots).

The Role of Ethics

So what happens at these atheist churches? Like atheists themselves, these congregations are freewheeling, diverse and democratic, answering to no higher authority, so it's dangerous to generalize too narrowly. But there are some broad similarities.

Nearly all of them contain some element of moral exhortation and celebration, teaching and preaching about the ethical values that humanists practice. The Sunday Assembly hosts humanist sermons on topics like the value of gratitude, or the importance of wonder. There's also usually music—for the Sunday Assembly, it's classic rock songs with a positive, humanist theme, like "Lean on Me" or "With a Little Help from My Friends," that the audience is invited to sing and clap along to. AJ Johnson, one of the main organizers and sponsors of the NYC Sunday Assembly, calls it "a radically inclusive, family-friendly celebration of life. We sing positive, popular songs, like 'Help!' by the Beatles. We listen to short, interesting talks. We meet new people." Most of them also organize community service and outreach projects.

The bigger question that needs to be answered—and the question that inevitably gets asked whenever these groups are discussed—is, why do atheists need these gatherings? Are they just a needless, misguided counterfeit of religion? Is it the case that "churches and ritualized worship . . . are best left to the people who feel the need to have a God figure in their lives"? Should nonbelievers be organized solely for "the purpose of repelling religious infringements on secular society" and nothing else?

The best answer to this is that the needs these congregations aim to fulfill aren't religious, but human. I grant that the term "atheist church" sounds clunky and self-contradictory, because these areas of human interaction have historically been claimed by religion and our language doesn't have good nonreligious words for them.

A Supportive Community

But whether atheist or theist, all human beings benefit from belonging to a welcoming, supportive community. Through congregations like this, we can help each other in times of need or crisis: when someone dies, we can gather to comfort the mourners and share memories of their life. We can come together to celebrate important life passages: for nonreligious people who want to get married, for example, we can offer a humanist celebrant to solemnize the wedding. We can also assemble to do good in the wider community, with charitable drives and volunteering (particularly important since religious organizations have a nasty habit of turning away atheists who want to help). Research has repeatedly affirmed the benefits of

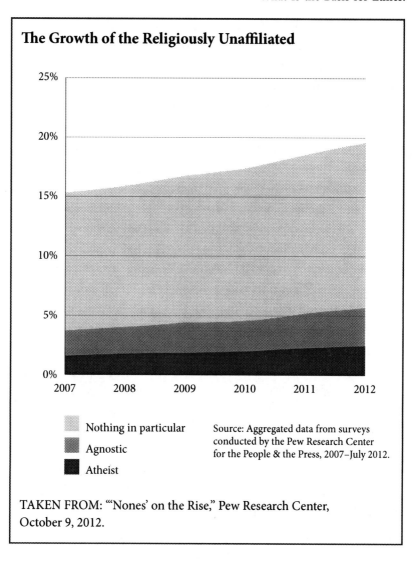

The Growth of the Religiously Unaffiliated

Nothing in particular

Agnostic

Atheist

Source: Aggregated data from surveys conducted by the Pew Research Center for the People & the Press, 2007–July 2012.

TAKEN FROM: "'Nones' on the Rise," Pew Research Center, October 9, 2012.

social connection, showing that belonging to a community contributes to leading longer, healthier, happier lives.

All this goes double for nonbelievers living in heavily religious communities. In places where there are few opportunities for friendship and social gathering outside a church, life as an atheist can be lonely and isolating. Nonreligious congregations restore this balance by offering a place where we can speak our minds freely, where we can find friends who think as we do, and where we can have invigorating conversations that don't have to begin by knocking down the same infuriating stereotypes every time. For all the benefits of online discussion, a merely virtual community can never fully substitute for that kind of joyous human contact and connection.

Besides the immediate tangible benefits, we also gather to affirm a common identity. In a society that's still majority religious, nonbelievers are frequently the targets of prejudice and misunderstanding (as in the story of the soup kitchen that turned away atheist volunteers). By organizing and becoming visible, we show the world who we are and what we value, and that's always the first step in fighting this kind of bigotry. It creates a positive and welcoming image of atheism that people will bear in mind when religious fundamentalists try to paint us with negative stereotypes about how we lack morals.

As AJ Johnson says, "I think the greatest value of Sunday Assembly is its appeal to people who may not call themselves atheists. Less than 3% of the population identifies as 'atheists.' However, about 14% of the population says 'Nothing in Particular.' This group is not being served by the current options. Helping these folks find a sense of 'belonging' should be an important goal for the entire nontheistic community, including self-identified atheists, agnostics and nones. Their acceptance helps fuels our own."

Personal experience bears this out. I've been to several of the New York City Sunday Assemblies, and they've all drawn a young, diverse crowd—parents and families, people of color, an almost equal mix of men and women, a broad spread of ages—that's very different from the bunch-of-crotchety-old-white-guys image that's often (and not always inaccurately) thought to be typical of atheism. It's clear that communities like this attract people who have little interest in atheist activism in the strictly political sense, people who just want to get on with their lives and live according to humanist values. As the numbers of nonreligious Americans continue to grow, we can be sure that these secular congregations will grow with them.

"We should acknowledge the religious sources of liberal secularism."

Remember the Religious Roots of Liberal Thought

Larry Siedentop

In the following viewpoint, Larry Siedentop argues that the Western world is having a moral crisis of identity. Siedentop contends that liberal secularism has gone too far in denying the moral content of its tradition and its religious roots. He claims that Christianity is at the source of the belief in equality and individual rights that underpins the morality of secular liberalism and that acknowledgement of this would strengthen the West's current position in the world. Siedentop is an emeritus fellow of Keble College, Oxford, and author of Inventing the Individual: The Origins of Western Liberalism.

As you read, consider the following questions:

1. According to Siedentop, the self-image of the Western world comes too close to equating liberal secularism with what?

2. The Christian movement challenged the understanding of society as what?

3. According to the author, the moral intuitions of Christianity founded on a belief in free will led to what kind of culture?

The West is in crisis. The advance of China, India and other nations has led to a dramatic shift of economic power. In the political sphere, military adventures in Iraq and Afghanistan have compromised Western influence, leading the US to draw back from its "superpower" role. Yet the West's troubles go deeper than that. It is suffering a moral crisis, a crisis of identity.

Some are now uncomfortable using the term "the West" for fear that it carries the residue of an imperialist and racist past. But that is not the only source of discomfort. The crisis of identity also springs from the challenge of Islam, a creed that can make Western liberal secularism seem morally tepid, if not worse. Indeed, the term "liberal" is at risk of becoming a pejorative. In continental Europe, it connotes little more than market economics. In parts of the US, it is becoming a synonym for "radical", or even "socialist".

But who are we, if not liberals? Elusive though it may at times be, this remains the best available description of Western attitudes and institutions. We lack a compelling account of their evolution, a story we can plausibly tell ourselves about our moral roots. Our self-image comes dangerously close to equating liberal secularism with nonbelief. A sophisticated version of that view is that our political and legal systems aim to achieve "neutrality". But that does not do justice to the moral content of our tradition.

Accounts of Western development usually involve a major discontinuity, captured in the phrase "the Middle Ages". Since the Renaissance and the Enlightenment, this period has been represented as one of superstition, social privilege and clerical oppression—the antithesis of liberal secularism. Historians have been tempted to maximise the moral and intellectual distance between the modern world and the Middle Ages, while minimising the moral and intellectual distance between modern Europe and antiquity.

Describing the ancient world as "secular"—with citizens free from the oppression of priests and an authoritarian church—became an important political weapon during early modern struggles to separate church and state in Europe. But this account fails to notice that the ancient family, the basic constituent of the city-state, was itself a kind of church. The paterfamilias was originally both the family's magistrate and high priest, with his wife, daughters and younger sons having a radically inferior status. Inequality remained the hallmark of the ancient patriarchal family. "Society" was understood as an association of families rather than of individuals.

It was the Christian movement that began to challenge this understanding. Pauline belief in the equality of souls in the eyes of God—the discovery of human freedom and its potential—created a point of view that would transform the meaning of "society". This began to undercut traditional inequalities of status. It was nothing short of a moral revolution, and it laid the foundation for the social revolution that followed. The individual gradually displaced the family, tribe or caste as the basis of social organisation.

This was a centuries-long process. By the 12th and 13th centuries, the papacy sponsored the creation of a legal system for the church, founded on the assumption of moral equality. Canon lawyers assumed that the basic organising unit of the legal system was the individual (or "soul"). Working from that assumption, canonists transformed the ancient doctrine of natural law ("everything in its place") into a theory of natural rights—the forerunner of modern liberal rights theory. By the 15th century, these intellectual developments contributed to a reform movement ("conciliarism") calling for something like representative government in the church.

The failure of that reform movement lay behind the outbreak of the Reformation, which led to religious wars and growing pressure across Europe for the separation of church and state. By the 18th century, such pressure had become a virulent anticlericalism, which reshaped the writing of Western history and with it our understanding of ourselves.

It is this selective memory of our past that lies behind our failure to see that it was moral intuitions generated by Christianity that were turned against the coercive claims of the church—intuitions founded on belief in free will, which led to the conclusion that enforced belief is a contradiction in terms. So it is no accident that the West generated a rights-based culture of principles rather than of rules. It is our enormous strength, reflected in the liberation of women and a refusal to accept that apostasy is a crime.

We should acknowledge the religious sources of liberal secularism. That would strengthen the West, making it better able to shape the conversation of mankind.

"Although morality is innate and processed by certain brain regions, it is relative and subject to influences by more primitive forces that at times overwhelm us."

Innate Morality Is Often Overwhelmed by Other Biological Processes

Srini Pillay

In the following viewpoint, Srini Pillay argues that although science supports the view that morality may be built into our nature, other systems work against our innate morality. Pillay claims that the moral network of the brain is often at odds with the "fear" network of the brain and the "craving" network. Pillay contends that although these competing systems do not influence what is right or wrong, understanding them is crucial to understanding how to behave morally. Pillay is the founder and chief executive officer of NeuroBusiness Group.

As you read, consider the following questions:

1. The author claims that the brain is hardwired for what kind of moral behavior?

2. How do unconscious fears affect moral behavior, according to Pillay?

3. The author contends that although the brain is wired for forgiveness, this is at odds with what other centers of the brain?

We all rely on morality to ensure a sense of safety for ourselves and society at large. Moral frameworks rely on what is "right" and "makes sense." Some blatantly protective examples are "it is wrong to murder" or "it is wrong to steal." These statements, however, stand in contrast to statements such as "do unto others as you would have them do unto you" where the moral sensibility is obvious but the actual follow-through rate is very low indeed. Why is the follow-through rate so low in certain cases, and what are the implications of this?

The Networks of the Brain

Brain imaging studies do in fact show that morality may be built into the nature of who we are—at a biological level. The studies show that the "accountant" of the brain that weighs risks and benefits is a central part of a network of brain regions involved in an innate moral predisposition. This brain region, the "ventromedial prefrontal cortex" (vmPFC) is highly connected to brain regions on the right side of the brain in what appears to be an "innate" manner that promotes behavior that takes the needs of others into consideration. We call the latter pro-social behavior.

While few people would argue that this innateness exists, the reason that I think that this argument falls short is that it ignores other brain systems that challenge this moral system. These other systems are very formidable indeed, and despite the innate morality we may have, these other brain regions may strongly influence the way we think and feel. Two of the greatest challenges to the moral network in the brain are the "fear" network and the "craving" network—both of which have automatic components that powerfully impact the moral brain.

The fear network comprising the amygdala as the lynchpin that connects to surrounding brain areas is so powerfully present in the human brain that it can register fears completely outside of awareness. In my book *Life Unlocked: 7 Revolutionary Lessons to Overcome Fear*, I have described how even blind people can identify fear—so impactful is its influence that you do not have to know that you have encountered it for it to turn on your brain's fear center. If we look at infidelity, prejudice and a host of other seemingly moralistic viewpoints, we can see that this fear center disrupts the processing of the brain's "accountant" and despite our innate moral predisposition, certain unconscious fears are likely to make you act in concert with this influence of your primitive fear-brain. You may struggle to have control over this, but much to your dismay be unable to do this.

The Obstacles to Morality

If for example you are afraid of losing your romantic partner or jealous of their relationships, you may in fact choose to have an affair because you seek control over this fear. In fact, men especially activate the amygdala when they are jealous. Also, if you fear certain races, you may become innately prejudiced against them. These responses are not without the input of social value systems in the brain and like moral reasoning, also interact with other brain regions. My argument here is that although morality is innate and processed by certain brain regions, it is relative and subject to influences by more primitive forces that at times overwhelm us.

Craving, similarly, is also strongly automatic and served by the primitive brain. And although it is subject to influences by the "thinking" brain, it is also granted a power of its own. The brain structures involved in craving are under the influence of the frontal lobe, but for many, this is only a weak connection. Thus, craving is also a formidable opponent to morality in the brain.

This has little to do with what is right or wrong for an individual or society. Being innate does not mean that something is "right." It simply means that the brain is wired to execute on a task more quickly and that this automatic response has been set down early on in life. The most profound argument that I would propose here is that we are also wired for forgiveness. A recent study showed that the brain's accountant on the left side is involved in forgiveness, but like the centers for morality, fear and craving, this region is also not independent of the desire to punish or anger centers of the brain.

The challenge in human existence then, is that our brain studies are showing us that the moral systems in the human brain live side by side with the formidable and often much more powerful systems for fear and craving and that the desire to forgive is also challenged by the desire for retribution. My point here is that these brain studies show that none of these ideas is absolute; that as human beings we are prone to a certain struggle of duality and opposites that live together in the brain, and that try as we may to restrain this, I do not believe that we can at the level of these systems. As [Albert] Einstein said: "You can never solve a problem on the level on which it was created"—which begs the question: If we are to solve this internal battle, what "level" can we access to do this?

Periodical and Internet Sources Bibliography

The following articles have been selected to supplement the diverse views presented in this chapter.

Vern L. Bengston	"Generation Atheist! Millennials to Religion—Get Out of Politics," *Salon*, November 4, 2013.
Sam Blumenfeld	"Secular Humanism: America's Establishment of Religion," *New American*, May 29, 2012.
Ross Douthat	"Ideas from a Manger," *New York Times*, December 21, 2013.
Kevin Drum	"Secular Ethics Are Doing Just Fine, Thank You Very Much," *Mother Jones*, December 22, 2013.
Selwyn Duke	"Nobel Laureate: World Needs 'Secular Ten Commandments' and Universal Values," *New American*, October 23, 2013.
David Hollenbach and Thomas A. Shannon	"A Balancing Act," *America*, March 5, 2012.
Wendy Kaminer	"Why Are Secular Businesses Claiming Religious Rights?," *Atlantic*, July 30, 2012.
Ed Kilgore	"The Secularist Agenda of the Christian Right," *Washington Monthly*, September 26, 2012.
Ross McCullough	"The Beauty of the Ethical," *First Things*, April 2011.
Nicholas P. Miller	"A Secular Threat," *Liberty*, September–October 2012.
Dave Niose	"Misinformation and Facts About Secularism and Religion," *Psychology Today*, March 30, 2011.
R.R. Reno	"The New Secular Moral Majority," *First Things*, December 2012.

OPPOSING
VIEWPOINTS®
SERIES

CHAPTER 2

What Ethics Should Guide Decisions About Life?

Chapter Preface

Many of the most socially divisive ethical issues center on actions involving the taking of life, such as in the cases of abortion and assisted suicide. The straightforward taking of innocent life—as in the murder of a person—is not generally considered morally controversial, but when the life involved is a fetus or one's own life, the answer is without consensus.

The moral debate about abortion frequently centers on the question of when life becomes morally relevant. There is little debate about the fact that a fetus, at some point at or shortly after conception, becomes a human life, in the sense of being a living creature with its own DNA. The question of moral relevance centers on the point at which this human life becomes a person, with moral rights. Life alone is not necessarily a morally relevant category: For example, plants are alive, but this would not appear to create a moral reason against destroying or eating them. The question about personhood appears to be one that will not be easily resolved; but even if agreement could be reached on the issue of personhood, abortion deals with a situation not readily mimicked elsewhere, since the fetus is inside the pregnant woman.

Assuming the fetus at some point prior to birth becomes a person, there is still the issue of determining when—if ever—a woman may take this life that is inside her. Although it may be noncontroversial that innocent persons should not be killed, women have rights to their own body that may or may not make the killing of a fetus morally permissible. An interesting case is where pregnancy will result in the death of the pregnant woman, as in this case it literally becomes one life against the other. In a pregnancy that results from rape, a pregnant woman can be said to have the fetus in her body quite unwillingly. Even those who find abortion morally repugnant in other cases often consider these two extreme cases morally permissible. Drawing the line between these cases and others, however, is not without difficulty. Did a woman whose birth control failed ask to be pregnant? Is this case like the rape case? If having a child will cause undue emotional or financial hardship, is this burden to the woman at all like the case that results in her death—the ultimate hardship? The issue of personhood in the abortion debate is only the start of the controversy. As these scenarios illustrate, pregnancy creates a situation without proper analogy elsewhere, where issues about the priority of an existing human person are pitted against those of a potential person or very new person.

The end of life, much like the beginning of life, also is fraught with ethical dilemmas. Euthanasia involves the taking of a life by another, as when a doctor gives a lethal injection to a terminally ill patient. Assisted suicide, by contrast, involves a doctor or another individual helping an individual take his or her own life. Aid in dying is a term that certain groups have developed to identify only cases of the latter that involve people who are already dying—those who are terminally ill and near the end of life—as a way of distinguishing it from more controversial cases. In all end-of-life cases, however, the moral dilemma revolves around an individual's moral right to take his or her own life and the morality of involvement by others. These cases differ from abortion by involving the consent of the person being killed, and the debate centers on the moral relevance of this consent.

The debates about abortion and assisted suicide illustrate the ripe moral dilemmas surrounding issues of taking life. As the authors in the following chapter illustrate, there are widely divergent views about the morality of these actions.

| *"Abortion might be the most inscrutable*
| *cultural issue of our time."*

There Is Wide Disagreement About the Morally Relevant Moment of Life

Kenneth W. Krause

In the following viewpoint, Kenneth W. Krause argues that the ongoing controversy about abortion illustrates the problems with defining the morally relevant features of human life. Krause claims that both the viability and conception of the fetus are problematic points of moral relevance. In addition, Krause contends that the balancing of rights of the woman and fetus does not resolve the moral issues about abortion. Finally, Krause argues that objection to abortion based on psychological pain of the mother and physical pain of the fetus is also problematic. Krause is a contributing editor for the Humanist *and a contributing editor and columnist for the* Skeptical Inquirer.

As you read, consider the following questions:

1. According to the author, in what US Supreme Court case was the right of privacy first identified?

Kenneth W. Krause, "Abortion's Still Unanswered Questions," *Humanist*, vol. 71, no. 4, July/August 2011, pp. 40–42. Copyright © 2011 by Kenneth W. Krause. All rights reserved. Reproduced by permission.

2. The author cites a philosophy professor who identifies what problem with the view of conception as the morally relevant dividing line of life?

3. Beginning in the 1980s, according to Krause, what two kinds of pain were put forth as being morally relevant to the abortion issue?

For thoughtful persons uncorrupted by religious or political agendas, abortion remains a complex topic implicating tough legal, philosophical, and scientific questions. How should we characterize the fetus, for example—as part of the mother or as a separate human being? Which has superior rights? Is the "right to privacy" constitutionally defensible? If so, was the trimester system outlined in *Roe v. Wade* the most prudent approach to balancing the woman's right against the state's legitimate interests? Is abortion really about something else altogether?

The Right of Privacy

The jurisprudence of abortion is highlighted in Erwin Chemerinsky's wide-ranging liberal rallying cry, *The Conservative Assault on the Constitution.* Founding dean of the law school at the University of California, Irvine, Chemerinsky admits the right of privacy was never expressed in the Constitution's text. Nor was it compelled by the Fourteenth Amendment's equal protection clause, for example, as was the landmark ruling in *Brown v. Board of Education.*

Nonetheless, *Roe's* revolutionary 1973 holding was not without precedent, loosely defined. The right of privacy was created—or "revealed," as some might prefer—eight years earlier in *Griswold v. Connecticut* where the Supreme Court struck a law prohibiting the use of contraceptives by married couples. Writing for the court, Justice William Douglas notoriously discovered the now fundamental right among the supposed "penumbras" emanating from the Bill of Rights—a still troublesome expression omitted from Chemerinsky's account.

Then, in the 1972 decision of *Eisenstadt v. Baird*, the court extended its more restrictive ruling in *Griswold* to cover all couples. Here, Chemerinsky accentuates the operative language: "If the right of privacy means anything," Justice William Brennan pronounced, "it is the right of the individual . . . to be free from unwarranted governmental intrusion into matters so fundamentally affecting a person as the decision whether to bear or beget a child."

Such was *Roe*'s immediate constitutional foundation, however one values it. But the privacy right's roots run deeper yet. In 1923 and 1925, respectively, the court toppled laws forbidding the teaching of German (*Meyer v. Nebraska*) and proscribing parochial school education (*Pierce v. Society of Sisters*). In 1942 the court invalidated a law mandating sterilization of certain criminals (*Skinner v. Oklahoma*) and, in 1967, a statute prohibiting interracial marriage (*Loving v. Virginia*).

In each case, the court concocted specific constitutional rights never enumerated in the founding document: to marry, procreate, and raise children. So "it was clear at the time of *Roe*," Chemerinsky argues, "that the Constitution had long been interpreted as protecting basic aspects of personal autonomy," especially those relating to family. Thus, he concludes, it's actually the textualists and not the supporters of *Roe* who urge radical changes in constitutional law.

The Relevance of Viability

The author completely disregards other obvious questions. Why should the right to procreate imply a right not to do so following a woman's decision to risk pregnancy? Are there any theoretical limits whatsoever to substantive due process and the right of privacy? Can we the people ever know those limits, except through judicial intervention or an unlikely constitutional amendment?

Even if we accept the right's authenticity, we still must consider the state's rationale for intruding on behalf of the fetus. In *Roe*, Justice Harry Blackmun located a compelling government interest at the point of viability "because the fetus then presumably has the capability of meaningful life outside the mother's womb." To fix the initiation of human life at conception, Chemerinsky concurs, would be to inappropriately base the law "not on consensus or science, but on religious views."

But is viability a distinction without a difference? Inside or outside the womb, after all, a "viable" fetus still requires intensive care. Unfortunately, the author never considers a much simpler and more traditional option—the moment of birth. Thus, cautious readers are left wondering whether scientific advances might soon render viability a confusingly fluid standard on the one hand, or if the glaring arbitrariness of *Roe*'s trimester system could have been avoided on the other.

The Problem with the Moment of Conception

So if sustainability and bright-line clarity are crucial, some skeptics might ask, why not choose the "moment" of conception? In *The Fetal Position: A Rational Approach to the Abortion Issue*, University of Southern Mississippi professor of philosophy and religion Chris Meyers challenges the very definability of that moment.

The problem, he contends, is that conception is a "gradual process with many steps extended over several hours." When the sperm first breaches the egg, for example, the latter has yet to divide a second time and still holds forty-six chromosomes. Even after meiosis, it takes about twelve hours for the DNA of both cells to completely fuse, and another eighteen for the zygote to begin dividing.

So at what precise point would the antiabortionist fix conception? Meyers asks us to imagine a newly invented but hardly inconceivable birth control pill. It doesn't thwart ovulation or prevent sperm from entering the uterus or egg cell. It only precludes dissolution of the sperm's head and, thus, the intermingling of parental DNA. Is the pill contraceptive or abortive? The antiabortionist can either admit he doesn't know when morally significant life begins, or designate an arbitrary point in developmental time as the moment of conception.

The rarefied details of abnormal development are no less exasperating. When, for instance, does life—and thus ensoulment, for the religionist—commence for the second of two identical twins who doesn't exist until several days following fertilization? Do conjoined twins possess separate lives and souls even though many share vital organs, including brains, and couldn't survive if separated? Does the genetic chimera—one human fused from two fertilized embryos—have one soul or two and, if only one, where did the second soul go?

"Instead of identifying what makes humans morally special with what makes us biologically alive," Meyers argues, "we would do better by identifying it with that which makes us persons: consciousness, the capacity for rational thought, the ability to have human feelings," and self-awareness. The philosophical waters begin to clear, in other words, only when one abandons the supernatural association of ensoulment with moral significance.

The Problem with Balancing Rights

In any case, let's assume two human beings with conflicting metaphysical interests. Which attendant liberty interest should prevail—the mother's right to control her body, or the fetus's right to life? One might presume life—the right on which all others depend—to reign supreme. But not so fast, warns the author. What if the human seeking life can achieve it only at the expense of the human seeking bodily control?

Meyers begins with Judith Thomson's legendary violinist hypothetical. You wake up in a hospital, the scenario goes, to find a supremely talented and thus valuable musician hooked up to your kidneys. You never consented to this burdensome union, but, if unplugged, the helpless violinist would perish. So far, the problem is relatively simple—you owe no duty to the musician or her adoring fans. So far, however, the analogy applies only to pregnant women who were raped.

But what if you bear partial responsibility for your predicament? Maybe you attended a party for the ailing violinist, Meyers continues, knowing that someone with your blood type might be drugged and recruited to the musician's cause. No problem—we would still acknowledge your right to bodily integrity. The same reasoning would apply if you invited a homeless stranger into your house on a very cold day and later decided to evict her. The initial kindness would not imply a continuing duty to shelter and feed.

Sure, but what if the stranger was your child? You have "the right to be selfish when it comes to your own body," Meyers resolves, "and no one can force you to let another use it." Likewise, so long as the fetus is not viable, "the pregnant woman has the right to deny the fetus the use of her body, even if that means the fetus dies."

Convinced? Rights comparisons resemble religious quarrels in their regrettable tendency toward insoluble emotional conflict. There must be a more rational way to resolve the predicament. What if the prevailing developmental science, for example, confirmed that no one capable of actually experiencing harm is injured during an abortion? Perhaps then we could broach more practical considerations, like the extent to which individual, family, and even national and international finances might be affected by compulsory childbirth.

The Issue of Pain

Which carries us to the issue of fetal pain. In *Ourselves Unborn: A History of the Fetus in Modern America*—easily the most sophisticated and engaging title of the three—Williams

Jack Corbett, "Life Begins at Conceptualization!," CartoonStock.com.

College historian Sara Dubow describes how the valuation of fetal life since the late nineteenth century has varied vis-à-vis intensely fought debates over gender roles and the relative authority of science and religion.

The post-*Roe* era was distinctly marked by the aforementioned disputes over conflicting rights. But beginning in the 1980s, two new claims—that women were psychologically traumatized by and that fetuses experienced terrible pain during abortion procedures—were woven together into a novel rhetorical strategy culminating in a popular, though conspicuously political, patriarchal, and antiscientific, "compassionate" conservatism.

In their mission statement emphasizing both physical and emotional injury to mothers, Americans United for Life [AUL] labeled abortion a "violent deception" producing two victims. AUL's list of legislative objectives featured a mandate that clinics "protect the health and safety of women" and "inform women of the health risks of abortion including the link between abortion and breast cancer." Similarly, the National Right to Life Committee circulated pamphlets warning women that, in addition to cancer, abortion can trigger "guilt, regret, divorce, promiscuity, child abuse, lesbianism, eating disorders, reckless behavior, substance abuse, and suicide."

In his 1984 address to the National Religious Broadcasters convention, President Ronald Reagan insisted that "[m]edical science doctors confirm that when the lives of the unborn are snuffed out, they often feel pain, pain that is long and agonizing." In response, Dr. Bernard Nathanson produced and narrated *The Silent Scream*, a graphic, twenty-eight minute videotape of an abortion procedure performed on a twelve-week-old fetus, which resurfaced in the 1990s during congressional debates over late-term ("partial-birth") abortion.

All of this proved emotionally rousing, to say the least. But the sober facts, Dubow reminds us, supported precious little of it. The American College of Obstetricians and Gynecologists knew of "no legitimate scientific information" in support of early pregnancy fetal pain. Certain prerequisites to discomfort, including a mature cerebellum, brain and spinal cord mylenization, and neurotransmitter hormones, were absent. Leading neurologists instructed as well that twelve-week-old fetuses lack the necessary nerve cell circuitry. The National Cancer Institute and the American Psychological Association were equally incredulous about the alleged links to breast cancer and postabortion trauma.

An Ongoing Controversy

Nevertheless, such propaganda would permeate debates in Congress and, eventually, the Supreme Court over late-term abortion procedures. In 2007 Justice Anthony Kennedy penned the majority opinions in *Gonzales v. Planned Parenthood* and *Gonzales v. Carhart* upholding the constitutionality of the

Partial-Birth Abortion [Ban] Act of 2003. Therein, he presumed to shield fetuses from the "brutal and inhumane" dilation and extraction procedure and to protect women from the "[s]evere depression and loss of esteem" that follows.

In her dissent, Justice Ruth Bader Ginsburg first noted the glaring scientific reality gap and then scolded Kennedy for perpetuating what she deemed an embarrassingly antiquated ideology. *Gonzales*, she concluded, "reflects ancient notions about women's place in the family that have long since been discredited." But as Dubow suggests, opposition to abortion has always been less about saving lives than preserving a cultural norm at the expense of its emerging and somewhat ill-defined alternative.

Indeed, abortion might be the most inscrutable cultural issue of our time. Its current party politics are especially maddening. Republicans tend to base their stance on particular religious tenets, the implementation of which would be both morally and constitutionally amiss. Democrats, by contrast, seem confused at best—frequently confessing both their support for choice and their heartfelt desire to reduce the number of abortions. But why the latter? What do they suppose is wrong with abortion?

| *"Not just for its own sake but for evaluating many ethical dilemmas, consciousness science is a vital field."*

When Do We Become Truly Conscious? The New Science of Consciousness Should Change How We Think About Thorny Ethical Dilemmas

Daniel Bor

In the following viewpoint, Daniel Bor argues that research about consciousness can inform numerous ethical debates, including abortion and animal rights. Bor contends that signs of advanced consciousness, such as self-awareness and metacognition, can be used to evaluate many moral dilemmas. Bor is a cognitive neuroscientist at the Sackler Centre for Consciousness Science at the University of Sussex, United Kingdom, and the author of The Ravenous Brain: How the New Science of Consciousness Explains Our Insatiable Search for Meaning.

As you read, consider the following questions:

1. According to Bor, on a personal level, what is consciousness?

2. Bor contends that it is highly unlikely that consciousness arises in a fetus until what stage of pregnancy?

3. According to the author, which animals pass the self-awareness test?

It is easy to view consciousness as a kind of magic. In religion it is represented by the mysterious soul, and in science the concept of consciousness at first appears quite alien. But many fields, such as the study of what distinguishes life from nonlife, had their earlier magical states eroded by careful scientific study. Consciousness is in the midst of a similar revolution.

The Nature of Consciousness

The investigation of our own awareness is a blossoming scientific field, where experiments are illuminating exciting details about this most intimate of scientific subjects. In my book *The Ravenous Brain*, I describe the latest consciousness science and how we are closing in on establishing a consciousness meter—a way to measure levels of awareness in any being that may be able to experience the world. Consciousness is in many ways the most important question remaining for science.

But the nature of consciousness is not just a vital question for science; it's also the source of some of society's thorniest, most fundamental ethical dilemmas.

On a personal level, consciousness is where the meaning to life resides. All the moments that matter to us, from falling in love to seeing our child's first smile, to that perfect holiday surrounded by snow-capped mountains, are obviously conscious events. If none of these events were conscious, if we weren't conscious to experience them, we'd hardly consider ourselves alive—at least not in any way that matters.

Whether I'm reveling in a glowing pleasure or even if I'm enduring a sharp sadness, I always sense that behind everything there is the privilege and passion of experience. Our consciousness is the essence of who we perceive ourselves to be. It is the citadel for our senses, the melting pot of thoughts, the welcoming home for every emotion that pricks or placates us. For us, consciousness simply is the currency of life.

Although some philosophers and scientists suspect that consciousness is a pointless side effect of cognitive processes, I believe the opposite: that our consciousness might indeed be responsible for our greatest intellectual achievements in both the arts and sciences. Whether our creativity and insight originates in our unconscious mind or not (I believe that the role of the unconscious has been overestimated), at the very least, our consciousness is the conduit to inspect these gems of inspiration and the driving force for turning them into reality.

The Point Where Consciousness Begins

It is not surprising, therefore, that questions about consciousness lie at the heart of many of our most fundamental ethical debates, one of which is abortion and the right to life. This is an appropriate point for me to play my proud father card. . . .

As a 2-year-old, Lalana runs around everywhere and has a vocabulary of a few hundred words. She can convey events to us that happened days or weeks before, usually because she is still so excited about them. She can also store wishes for the future. For instance, we might tell her offhand that when we get home, we'll play with making bubbles. Hours later, as soon as she enters the house, she'll run straight to the shelf with the bubble bottle and scream, "Bubbu! Bubbu!" She has a strong set of loves and hates, and her emotionally sensitive, passionate, cheeky, disturbingly stubborn personality is already pronounced.

Having prided myself on my objectivity throughout my adult life, I've embarrassingly found that my daughter is the main exception to this aim: I've not only been taken aback by how fiercely I love her but also by how proud I am of her and how quickly I distort the truth to make her seem exceptional in every way. But when I can step back from these views, I ask myself: At what point did she become conscious? Obviously she is conscious now, as she can tell me her inner thoughts via language. But when did she start experiencing her environment? On a personal, intuitive level, I had little doubt that her first intense bursts of laughter at my silly antics, when she was a few months old, reflected a substantive consciousness. But was she conscious well before this? Was she aware when she was still in the womb, kicking away? Or could she only experience things when she first opened her eyes to the outside world on the day of her birth?

The Consciousness of a Fetus

Finding answers to these questions isn't merely a matter of curiosity. In the United States, people have been murdered for carrying out abortions. In many other countries, abortion is illegal even if the woman has been raped, and some prominent U.S. politicians, including Republican vice-presidential nominee Paul Ryan, support similarly harsh laws. Although such positions are usually determined by religion, a related mind-set is that fetuses are already conscious and even capable of feeling pain. Indeed, this has recently been the basis states have used to further restrict a woman's rights on this issue, with Arizona the latest state to join this group by disallowing abortions after 20 weeks.

But what does science have to say on this matter? The evidence is clear that a fetus can respond to sights, sounds, and smells, and it can even react to these by producing facial expressions. The evidence is equally clear, however, that these responses are generated by the most primitive parts of the brain, which are unconnected to consciousness, and therefore these actions don't in any way imply that the fetus is aware. Furthermore, the fetus is deliberately sedated by a series of chemicals produced by the placenta, so even if it had the capacity for consciousness, there is almost no chance that it could ever be conscious in the womb. Consequently, it can't consciously feel pain.

But what if the fetus is removed from the womb and its sleep-inducing chemicals? Will the fetus suddenly be conscious in the outside world? In adult humans, for normal consciousness to occur, it is now generally agreed that two sets of regions need to be intact, functional, and able to communicate effectively with one another: the thalamus, a kind of relay station in the middle of the brain that connects many regions with many others; and the prefrontal parietal network, our most high-level, general purpose section of cortex. If either the thalamus or prefrontal parietal network is substantially damaged, the patient is likely to enter into a vegetative state, with virtually no sign of consciousness.

When do these brain regions form in the growing fetus? Only after about 29 weeks are the connections between these areas properly laid out, and it takes another month or so before the thalamus and the rest of the cortex are effectively communicating, as revealed by brain waves. So it's highly unlikely that consciousness, at least in any form that we'd recognize as human awareness, arises before about 33 weeks into pregnancy. There are therefore no scientific reasons for restricting abortion on the grounds that the fetus will experience pain, at least until very late in pregnancy. This evidence has heavily influenced my views here, and consequently I am very much pro-choice.

The Consciousness of Animals

Another ethical issue that hinges on questions of consciousness is that of animal rights. Every person on the planet, on average, consumes twice his or her weight in animal-derived food each year. Food production, as well as animal experimentation, could be causing the suffering of many millions of animals yearly.

If no animals except humans have consciousness, there's no problem, as suffering requires consciousness. But if even those animals classically assumed to have very limited mental faculties, such as poultry and fish, have a substantive awareness and significant capacity for suffering, then are we justified in inflicting all this pain and discomfort on them?

If science could come up with some means of testing for the presence of consciousness in other animals and perhaps also a way of gauging the extent of consciousness when it's found, this would have a huge impact on all ethical spheres of the animal rights debate.

On the surface, because animals can't use language to tell us they are conscious, this seems an intractable problem. But a surprising amount of evidence has emerged that addresses the question of animal consciousness. For a start, we can ask which other species have brain regions similar to those we know are critical for human consciousness, namely the thalamus and prefrontal parietal network. Most mammals share these structures with us in some form, suggesting strongly that they too have some significant levels of consciousness. But this is a problematic approach, ignoring the possibility that very distant species independently evolved the capacity for consciousness. For instance, crows can use a series of tools to hook a juicy grub, and octopuses can open a screw-on lid to a jar to retrieve a tasty crab. Although these animals have no cortex, they appear to demonstrate a mental life that many would classify as conscious.

The most prominent scientific theories of consciousness are converging on the idea that it is related to a certain kind of information processing, in which multiple strands of data are drawn together, and that it is dependent on a certain kind of network architecture. Arguably the most popular theory along these lines, information integration theory by Giulio Tononi, effectively assumes that consciousness is a continuum across the animal kingdom. If so, even the lowly nematode worm, with a few hundred neurons, will have some, albeit minimal, level of consciousness. If something approximating this theory proves correct, it has huge implications for our relationship to all animals on the planet.

The Signs of Advanced Consciousness

But even if we assume that there is a continuum of consciousness, this is of limited use in helping answer questions of animal rights. For instance, a worm may indeed have a capacity for *some* consciousness, but the way it experiences the world may be infinitesimally limited compared to human awareness. More pertinent for ethics is the scientific exploration of whether other animals have advanced forms of consciousness, such as self-awareness. This can be tested using the mirror test: A spot of paint is placed on an animal's face, and it is then presented with a mirror. Many animals will simply attack or try to escape from the apparent foe in the mirror, but a select few will recognize themselves, as demonstrated by them trying to remove or at least examine the strange spot. The current list of animals that clearly pass this test includes chimpanzees, orangutans, gorillas, dolphins, elephants, pigs (on a modified version of the test), and even magpies. But this list of species is sure to grow as more animals are tested in ways that are most appropriate for them.

Another marker of an advanced consciousness is something called metacognition, the ability to be aware of your own mind and report on it, for instance by saying: "I'm sure I saw that cat in the woods," or "You might have seen a cat, but I didn't spot anything." In human experiments, it is seen as definitive evidence of consciousness. But we are not the only species to have this skill.

Metacognition in other species is usually measured using a gambling task: An animal makes a decision about a stimulus and can then press either a high-risk button that promises a large food reward if the decision was correct but food restriction if it was wrong, or a low-risk button with a meager reward regardless of whether the animal is right or wrong. If the animal has significant metacognition—in other words, if it knows whether it is just guessing or if it has solid knowledge about a given stimulus—then it should usually press the high-risk button when it knows the correct answer and the low-risk one when it's wrong. This is exactly what several other species, including the great apes and monkeys, do. These species demonstrate an advanced form of consciousness that in humans is definitive evidence of our awareness.

The Relevance of Consciousness Research

My take on all this data is that it is extremely likely that all the species that can recognize themselves in the mirror or show metacognitive abilities have an advanced form of consciousness. But for any species that hasn't yet passed these tests, we simply don't know whether they lack the ability or just haven't been tested appropriately. The cautious attitude, I believe, is to assume that all mammals and the octopus at the very least, but possibly many more species, have a significant capacity for consciousness.

Consequently, I am a vegetarian, as are several prominent consciousness researchers. I believe it would be ethically consistent for us to extend our own rights to life and freedom from torture to any species that can recognize itself in the mirror, show clear metacognition, or even demonstrate extensive tool use. Barring all these animals from the food industry and passing laws to protect them based on their consciousness would be a radical step and not one that I can see any political leader advocating any time soon. Nevertheless, it would be a consistent and caring departure from the way much of society currently views animals, and it would acknowledge the advances in our scientific understanding of the mental lives of these other species.

Consciousness research informs other political issues as well. For instance, how can we assess the level of consciousness remaining in someone who has suffered severe brain damage and is in a vegetative state? At what point should we let such patients die? And it is possible that in the decades to come, we might also need to start thinking about how we assess artificial forms of consciousness and what rights we consequently need to bestow on such beings.

Therefore, not just for its own sake but for evaluating many ethical dilemmas, consciousness science is a vital field. Anyone interested in key political debates may want to keep a close eye on its progress in the years to come.

"We have no obligation to allow every being with the potential to become a rational being to realize that potential."

The Choice of a Pregnant Woman Always Outweighs the Life of a Fetus

Peter Singer

In the following viewpoint, Peter Singer argues that bans on abortion in the developing world lead to many unnecessary deaths. Singer claims that opponents of abortion make the mistake of conflating membership in the human species with an ethical right to life. Singer contends that a woman's interests always outweigh any supposed interests of a fetus. Singer is professor of bioethics at Princeton University, laureate professor at the University of Melbourne, and author of Practical Ethics.

As you read, consider the following questions:

1. According to Singer, what percentage of the world's abortions occur in developing countries?

2. The author cites a World Health Organization study finding that unsafe abortions lead to the deaths of how many women each year?

3. According to Singer, the legalization of abortion in South Africa led to how much of a drop in abortion-related deaths?

In the Dominican Republic last month [July 2012], a pregnant teenager suffering from leukemia had her chemotherapy delayed, because doctors feared that the treatment could terminate her pregnancy and therefore violate the nation's strict antiabortion law. After consultations between doctors, lawyers, and the girl's family, chemotherapy eventually was begun, but not before attention had again been focused on the rigidity of many developing countries' abortion laws.

Abortion in the Developing World

Abortion receives extensive media coverage in developed countries, especially in the United States, where Republicans have used opposition to it to rally voters. Recently, President Barack Obama's reelection campaign counterattacked, releasing a television advertisement in which a woman says that it is "a scary time to be a woman," because Mitt Romney has said that he supports outlawing abortion.

But much less attention is given to the 86% of all abortions that occur in the developing world. Although a majority of countries in Africa and Latin America have laws prohibiting abortion in most circumstances, official bans do not prevent high abortion rates.

In Africa, there are 29 abortions per 1,000 women, and 32 per 1,000 in Latin America. The comparable figure for Western Europe, where abortion is generally permitted in most circumstances, is 12. According to a recent report by the World Health Organization [WHO], unsafe abortions lead to the deaths of 47,000 women every year, with almost all of these deaths occurring in developing countries. A further five million women are injured each year, sometimes permanently.

Almost all of these deaths and injuries could be prevented, the WHO says, by meeting the need for sex education and information about family planning and contraception, and by providing safe, legal induced abortion, as well as follow-up care to prevent or treat medical complications. An estimated 220 million women in the developing world say that they want to prevent pregnancy, but lack either knowledge of, or access to, effective contraception.

Access to Legal Abortion

That is a huge tragedy for individuals and for the future of our already very heavily populated planet. Last month, the London Summit on Family Planning, hosted by the British government's Department for International Development and the [Bill & Melinda] Gates Foundation, announced commitments to reach 120 million of these women by 2020.

The Vatican newspaper responded by criticizing Melinda Gates, whose efforts in organizing and partly funding this initiative will, it is estimated, lead to nearly three million fewer babies dying in their first year of life, and to 50 million fewer abortions. One would have thought that Roman Catholics would see these outcomes as desirable. (Gates is herself a practicing Catholic who has seen what happens when women cannot feed their children, or are maimed by unsafe abortions.)

Restricting access to legal abortion leads many poor women to seek abortion from unsafe providers. The legalization of abortion on request in South Africa in 1998 saw abortion-related deaths drop by 91%. And the development of the drugs misoprostol and mifepristone, which can be provided by pharmacists, makes relatively safe and inexpensive abortion possible in developing countries.

The Antiabortion Fallacy

Opponents will respond that abortion is, by its very nature, unsafe—for the fetus. They point out that abortion kills a

Global and Regional Estimates of Induced Abortion, 2008

Region	Number of Abortions (millions)	Abortion Rate (abortions per 1,000 women aged 15–44)		
	2008	1995	2003	2008
World	43.8	35	29	28
Developed countries	6.0	39	25	24
Excluding Eastern Europe	3.2	20	19	17
Developing countries	37.8	34	29	29
Excluding China	28.6	33	30	29
Africa	6.4	33	29	29
Asia	27.3	33	29	28
Europe	4.2	48	28	27
Latin America	4.4	37	31	32
Northern America	1.4	22	21	19
Oceania	0.1	21	18	17

Original Source: Sedgh G et al., Induced abortion: incidence and trends worldwide from 1995 to 2008, *Lancet*, 2012.

TAKEN FROM: Guttmacher Institute, "Facts on Induced Abortion Worldwide," January 2012.

unique, living human individual. That claim is difficult to deny, at least if by "human" we mean "member of the species *Homo sapiens*."

It is also true that we cannot simply invoke a woman's "right to choose" in order to avoid the ethical issue of the moral status of the fetus. If the fetus really did have the moral status of any other human being, it would be difficult to argue that a pregnant woman's right to choose includes the right to bring about the death of the fetus, except perhaps when the woman's life is at stake.

The fallacy in the antiabortion argument lies in the shift from the scientifically accurate claim that the fetus is a living individual of the species *Homo sapiens* to the ethical claim that the fetus therefore has the same right to life as any other human being. Membership of the species *Homo sapiens* is not enough to confer a right to life on a being. Nor can something like self-awareness or rationality warrant greater protection for the fetus than for, say, a cow, because the fetus has mental capacities that are inferior to those of cows. Yet "pro-life" groups that picket abortion clinics are rarely seen picketing slaughterhouses.

We can plausibly argue that we ought not to kill, against their will, self-aware beings who want to continue to live. We can see this as a violation of their autonomy, or a thwarting of their preferences. But why should a being's potential to become rationally self-aware make it wrong to end its life before it actually has the capacity for rationality or self-awareness?

We have no obligation to allow every being with the potential to become a rational being to realize that potential. If it comes to a clash between the supposed interests of potentially rational but not yet even conscious beings and the vital interests of actually rational women, we should give preference to the women every time.

| *"Abortion advocates are laying a 'moral'*
| *groundwork for murder."*

How the Left's Abortion Thinking Led to Gosnell

Benjamin Brophy

In the following viewpoint, Benjamin Brophy argues that the pro-choice view that life does not begin at conception has led to thinking that justifies immoral actions. Brophy contends that the actions of convicted abortion physician Kermit Gosnell for the murders of babies born alive is a natural consequence of the line of thinking that privileges a woman's right to choose over the life of a fetus. Brophy is the director of new media and visual communications for the American Spectator.

As you read, consider the following questions:

1. The author, in objecting to a pro-choice advocate's argument, claims that the death penalty is not similar to abortion in what way?

2. The author claims that ultimately the pro-choice view is simply an extension of what moral view?

3. Brophy argues that the Left's moral position privileges what over the lives of children?

With the horrors of Kermit Gosnell in full view, it is time we start investigating some of the critical thinking by the Far Left on the issue of abortion. These ethical presuppositions have created necessary, but not sufficient circumstances for an atrocity like Gosnell's to occur. As such, they deserve discussion and rebuke.

Mary Elizabeth Williams wrote at Salon.com some weeks back about her belief that life does begin at conception, but that has never stopped her from being pro-choice. Her piece is an excellent representation of what thought extremes the pro-choice lobby is headed towards:

> Here's the complicated reality in which we live: All life is not equal. That's a difficult thing for liberals like me to talk about, lest we wind up looking like death-panel-loving, kill-your-grandma-and-your-precious-baby storm troopers. Yet a fetus can be a human life without having the same rights as the woman in whose body it resides. She's the boss. Her life and what is right for her circumstances and her health should automatically trump the rights of the non-autonomous entity inside of her. Always.

So, and I hope I am summing her position up fairly, Williams believes that human life does begin at conception, but that not all life is equal in value. Some life is worth taking for the benefit of other lives.

She points to choices the U.S. government makes regarding drone strikes, the death penalty, euthanasia, and people being taken off life support. Indeed, it is an interesting cavalcade of life decisions we as society face on a regular basis.

I'll try to deal with each in short. Regarding drone strikes, for the sake of argument, I'll cede that the death of innocent men, women, and children as "collateral damage" is wrong and should end. However, pointing to another evil to justify your personal preference of what lives are more valuable than others does not justify your original premise. In terms of the death penalty, what crimes have the 50 million aborted children (as Williams defines fetuses since life begins at conception according to her) committed? Right-to-die laws in certain states are the result of the individual's wish to end their own lives. Are our children offered the same opportunity in utero?

Finally, she cites the decision to take individuals off life support. This does have something compelling in common with abortion. An individual on life support cannot live on his or her own power. This is true for babies in utero . . . to a point. Children as young as 22 weeks can live independently from their mothers. So instantly, Williams should be ready to end all abortions after that point, but of course, she is not. But further, a person on life support has no long-term prognosis of improvement (barring a miracle). If families had the same chance for their family member to survive as a baby being born alive, they would certainly hold out. It is in the face of no hope that these difficult decisions are made.

Williams must have drawn many of her conclusions from Peter Singer, "moral" philosopher. Singer stated in his book [Rethinking] Life and Death that the argument that a fetus is not human life

> is a resort to a convenient fiction that turns an evidently living being into one that legally is not alive. Instead of accepting such fictions, we should recognize that the fact that a being is human, and alive, does not in itself tell us whether it is wrong to take that being's life.

Singer, like Williams, holds that the taking of some lives for the benefit of other lives may not be morally wrong. This is it, this is the deep crux of the matter for the Far Left. It is their contention that taking a life because it inconveniences another human being is not wrong.

Assuming that philosophical position, how is what Kermit Gosnell did incongruent with the positions these two liberals

The Debate About Personhood

The debate about "personhood" is really the debate about who will be included in the human community, who will be respected, and who will receive legal protection. This debate goes back over the centuries, throughout which various classes of human beings were excluded from the human family. Those excluded tend to change over time but have been at various points Native Americans, Africans, Catholics in Protestant-dominated countries, Protestants in Catholic-dominated countries, non-Muslims, Jews, the handicapped, and women. Every single time we've said, this or that class of human beings does not merit protection and respect, I think we've made a terrible mistake. Today, I believe we're making another terrible mistake in excluding from full protection and respect human beings prior to birth.

Christopher Kaczor as told to Kathryn Jean Lopez,
"Pro-Life Aristotle," National Review Online,
October 19, 2011.

have staked out? Indeed, the only instances with which they may quibble were the abortions Gosnell performed against his patients' wills. But as for the rest, his actions remain logically consistent with their positions.

And that should terrify us.

Singer apparently has set quite the example for his former place of employ, Monash University, where two professors have taken up his moral equivalence on life.

Alberto Giubilini with Monash University in Melbourne and Francesca Minerva at the Centre for Applied Philosophy and Public Ethics at the University of Melbourne write that in "circumstances occur[ing] after birth such that they would have justified abortion, what we call after-birth abortion should be permissible."

These ideas, these precepts are dangerous. If there is a silver lining to the Gosnell case, it is the clear and brutal evidence of what high-minded "ethical thinking" like Singer's can lead to. Those who advocate for life need to aggressively insist upon calling this thinking for what it is; justification for Eichmann-like evil. Abortion advocates are laying a "moral" groundwork for murder.

And what is the reason for laying this groundwork? The fact that some babies are inconvenient.

Ultimately this is simply an extension of moral relativism. With moral concepts being completely unmoored from any absolute anchor, all principles revolve around individual perceptions. So to dig in and get a little less esoteric, an individual who is not emotionally or fiscally ready to have a child is willing to sacrifice a human life (or for the sake of argument, potential life) because raising a child would be hard, and why should she suffer because of a newer life? Is this what "freedom" has led us to? A complete disregard for anything that is not individually "beneficial"?

Horrifyingly, the arguments presented here all support that decision.

Some might argue that society sets up the expectations for the concept of life. You know, because we humans nailed that in Soviet Russia, Nazi Germany, the Spanish Inquisition, slavery, etc., etc. The Left may also argue that the overwhelming majority of abortions happen in the first trimester. So be it, we should be able to agree that legislation banning all abortions that happen after 21 weeks should be enacted. However, if that was even suggested, the Left would be apoplectic. That's because the moral assumptions underlying their position value personal freedom (for parents) over the life of children. If there is any chance for life, shouldn't we as a people fight for it? We go to great lengths to preserve any shred of life found outside the womb, why are we so malicious against life inside of one?

The conditions of Gosnell's clinic also prompt the question 'How many more clinics like this exist?' There are already reports of some. How could the freedom of consequence-free sex possibly be worth the price of children's lives? Those of us on the right have long been mocked for saying these arguments create slippery slopes that can lead to horrible immorality. Yet what is Gosnell but the reality of how dangerous moral relativism is?

The 'freedom to choose' is not worth the cost.

| "Human choice—the right to make important life decisions—is a part of the liberty and dignity that follow us all our lives, to our deaths."

Aid in Dying Is a Moral and Just Health Care Choice

Barbara Coombs Lee

In the following viewpoint, Barbara Coombs Lee argues that terminally ill individuals should be able to obtain medication to aid in dying and that such medical practice is morally distinct from assisted suicide. Lee contends that any religious objection to aid in dying should not extend into the legal sphere, but should remain limited in relevance to believers. Lee is president of Compassion & Choices, a nonprofit organization dedicated to expanding and protecting the rights of the terminally ill.

As you read, consider the following questions:

1. In what year did Washington State pass the Death with Dignity Act, which legalized aid in dying, according to Lee?

2. Who was the first and most vocal opponent to Oregon's movement for death with dignity in 1994, according to the author?

3. Lee argues that what fraction of Oregonians die under the provisions of that state's death with dignity law?

Compassion & Choices works to improve care and expand choice at the end of life. We dream of a time when all can live and die as free people—in dignity according to their own values and beliefs.

The Support for Aid in Dying

It's an interesting circumstance that the United States Conference of Catholic Bishops (USCCB) met in Washington State to adopt its first formal teaching on life-ending medication as an end-of-life choice. While this is a new attack, the Catholic hierarchy has a long, well-documented history of opposition to patient autonomy at the end of life. In 2008 Washington citizens passed a Death with Dignity Act by large margins. The Catholic Church's political arms were principal funders of the opposing campaign. Support for aid in dying is strong in every corner of the state, and Compassion & Choices of Washington is a highly respected partner with health care providers, churches and other institutions to improve end-of-life care, increase hospice utilization, and ensure access to and compliance with the Death with Dignity Act.

We are proponents of comprehensive end-of-life choices and defend our advocacy as compassionate, moral and just. Most Americans believe a mentally competent, terminally ill person should be able to obtain medication for peaceful dying from their physician. The Gallup organization has polled this question since 1947 and never found less than a solid majority in favor. Like the bishops meeting in Seattle today [June 17, 2011], we oppose assisting suicides, because suicide is the self-destructive impulse of a mentally ill person. Assisting a suicide is a felony in Washington and Oregon, and the Oregon legislature is expanding that felony to include mailing suicide kits into the state. A bright and wide line separates the crime of assisting a suicide from the medical practice of aid in dying. Blurring that line, or pretending it doesn't exist, does a tremendous disservice to terminally ill patients and to a society struggling to perfect end-of-life care.

The Catholic conference's battle against the medical practice of aid in dying has been vigorous, and it promotes an error of logic by lumping it together with the crime. Their position is not new, but we welcome—and are deeply grateful for—today's clarity and affirmation that religious objection is the foundation of opposition to the medical practice of aid in dying.

The Place of Religion

In 1994 Oregon's then archbishop [William] Levada was the first and most vocal opponent of the Oregon movement for death with dignity, and everyone understood opposition arose from a particular set of religious beliefs. In subsequent campaigns, religious arguments faded into the background. From 1995–2011 opponents concentrated on secular arguments. But 14 years of practice, volumes of medical research and diligent state oversight in Oregon and Washington have disproven every secular argument. No credible claim remains that aid in dying compromises end-of-life care; weakens hospices; threatens people with disabilities; discriminates against women, elders or vulnerable populations, or in fact harms anyone. So we are back to 1994. Only the arguments based on religious teaching remain intact, and the USCCB reinforces those teachings today.

We respect the role of the conference of bishops in affirming Catholic doctrine and guiding those of the Catholic faith. But we cannot accept that the instruction of one religious authority would overrule the most personal decisions of indi-

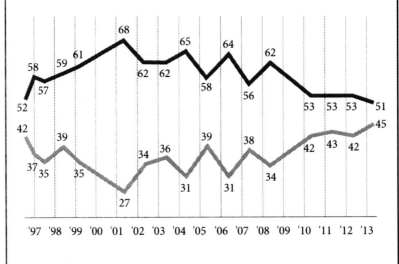

Support for Doctor-Assisted "Suicide"

When a person has a disease that cannot be cured and is living in severe pain, do you think doctors should or should not be allowed by law to assist the patient to commit suicide if the patient requests it?

■ Percent should

▨ Percent should not

TAKEN FROM: Gallup polls, 1997–2013.

viduals of every faith; not in a religiously diverse society. The choice of how to address suffering in a terminal illness must be the province of dying individuals themselves in consultation with their doctors, families, clergy and conscience. Our government has no place policing religious doctrine at the bedside of dying Americans.

The hierarchy of the Catholic Church uses its political and lobbying force across this nation to shape the law, limit patient choice and impose its teachings on all Americans. This year they led the campaign to overturn the Montana Supreme Court's decision affirming aid in dying for terminally ill Montanans. The policy statements adopted here by the bishops have practical consequences for every American. Their teachings govern Catholic health care providers and restrict the choices of all patients—Catholic or non-Catholic—who purchase Catholic health plans or enter Catholic institutions.

The Meaning of Compassion and Choice

The conference makes special note of the words in the name of our organization, which reflect our values. I'd like to set the record straight.

The conference's statements say our compassion focuses on eliminating patients, not suffering. No, our compassion focuses on providing comfort and peace of mind to individuals who fear they will suffer unbearably in their dying. Comfort and peace of mind come from obtaining, or knowing they could obtain, medication to bring about a peaceful death. Patients need not ingest the medication to achieve peace of mind. Every year, one in six dying Oregonians inquires about the death with dignity law. Only one in one thousand dies under its provisions. Few use the law, but many are comforted by it. The purpose of prescriptions written under the law is to provide comfort.

The conference's statements also say death with dignity laws restrict choice. This claim defies logic. Simply adding a health care choice in no way pressures people to exercise that choice. People feel comforted, not pressured; and safeguards in the law guarantee it remains this way.

Human choice—the right to make important life decisions—is a part of the liberty and dignity that follow us all our lives, to our deaths. The government in a civilized society, one that protects religious freedom, owes its people no less than that liberty and dignity.

"The case for allowing patients to choose medical aid in dying is strongly rooted in solid and widely shared ethical principles."

Physician-Assisted Dying Is Justified by Accepted Ethical Principles

Jean Mercier, Wayne Sumner, and Daniel Weinstock

In the following viewpoint, Jean Mercier, Wayne Sumner, and Daniel Weinstock argue that the principles of respect for autonomy and compassion for fellow citizens create the ethical case in favor of medical aid in dying. Mercier is a professor in the Department of Political Science at Université Laval, Quebec City, Canada. Sumner is professor emeritus in the Department of Philosophy at the University of Toronto, Canada, as well as the author of Assisted Death: A Study in Ethics and Law. *Weinstock is director of the Institute for Health and Social Policy and a professor in the Faculty of Law at McGill University, Montreal, Canada.*

As you read, consider the following questions:

1. According to the authors, opponents of aid in dying argue that it is morally wrong for the same reason that what other act is wrong?

2. The authors argue that respect for autonomy may be overlooked as an ethical principle for what reason?

3. According to the authors, murder is wrong due to what two factors?

On June 5, 2014, Bill 52 *An Act Respecting End-of-Life Care* became law in Quebec. With support for the bill extending across all of the major parties, a strong majority endorsed the legislation on medical aid in dying (94 votes to 22). This vote was preceded by several years of public debate. In 2009, the College of Medicine published a discussion paper on the subject. This paper prompted the creation of a legislative Select Committee to investigate the subject. The Select Committee examined both written and oral testimony for several months, and also undertook a fact-finding mission to Europe in 2011.

In the weeks preceding the vote, opponents of the bill stepped up their fight, utilizing arguments of widely varying quality. Some of those arguments are ethical, claiming that physician-assisted dying is simply wrong. This claim is usually supported by appeal to a principle of "the sanctity of life," which forbids the intentional killing of innocent persons. Physician-assisted dying is wrong, they argue, for the same reason that murder is wrong.

The Principles of Autonomy and Compassion

Our view is that, on the contrary, the case for allowing patients to choose medical aid in dying is strongly rooted in solid and widely shared ethical principles.

One of those principles is respect for the autonomy and self-determination of individuals, including the autonomy of patients at the end of life. This principle obliges us to respect the right of individuals to make their own decisions about their own lives. It is embodied in the different charters of rights and freedom in Canada and serves as the basis of most of our democratic institutions. The principle of autonomy already governs most other aspects of our lives. Bill 52 would simply extend it as well to the final stages of life, to decisions about their own care made by patients who are suffering during the dying process.

Respect for autonomy might be overlooked as an ethical principle only because it is so ingrained in our daily occupations that we take it for granted. But those whose liberty and self-determination are disregarded in countries all over the world can attest to its importance. It is thus not surprising that the extension of autonomy and freedom of choice to end-of-life treatment is only debated and considered in democratic, open societies.

The second ethical principle supporting physician-assisted dying is compassion for our fellow citizens. Although contemporary palliative medicine is capable of alleviating most suffering at the end of life, it cannot prevent all of it. Some patients will continue to experience unbearable physical symptoms or psychological distress despite the best that palliative care can offer. This suffering is unnecessary, since it can be prevented by allowing patients the option of medical aid in dying. Forcing patients to undergo unnecessary suffering is not compassionate but cruel.

Those who advocate for the legal option of medical aid in dying have been quite consistent in calling upon these two principles, autonomy and compassion, in support of their efforts.

The Meaning of Autonomy

The English word *autonomy* is a compound of the Greek word *autos* meaning "self" or "own," and *nomos*, meaning "law." Thus, in the original Greek, *autonomy* has the sense of (to give to) oneself one's laws, or perhaps, to make one's laws knowing that one is doing so. Contemporary usage of the word *autonomy* emerged in the eighteenth century, retaining a relation to the original Greek meaning but diverging in significant ways. Autonomy in contemporary usage is used synonymously with concepts such as freedom, liberty, and independence and is contrasted with concepts such as unfreedom, dependence, and heteronomy.

Tyler Krupp, "Autonomy,"
in Encyclopedia of Political Theory. *Vol. 1. Ed. Mark Bevir.*
Thousand Oaks, CA: SAGE Reference, 2010.

The Difference with Murder

It should now be obvious why the opponents' equation of physician-assisted dying with murder is mistaken. No one, of course, doubts that murder is wrong. But its wrongness is due to two important factors: the harm it does to the victim and its violation of the victim's autonomy. Neither of these factors applies to physician-assisted dying.

If a patient has made a voluntary request for medical aid in dying, having been fully informed of his prognosis and of all of the options available for end-of-life care, then a physician's willingness to comply with that request cannot compromise the patient's autonomy. Murder substitutes the will of the perpetrator for that of the victim. Physician-assisted dying respects the free will of the patient.

Murder harms its victims by depriving them of further life which would be of value to them. But patients elect medical aid in dying when the only future they can foresee promises nothing but additional suffering. In their own view of it, a continuation of life would have no value for them. Far from harming them, a physician-assisted death would be a benefit for them.

There is therefore no analogy between medical aid in dying and cases of unjustified homicide. In light of that, there is no ethical case against a law which would provide dying patients with this option. And there is a very strong ethical case in favour of it.

VIEWPOINT 7

> *"Euthanasia raises the fundamental question of whether our culture will retain the moral capacity to sustain a culture of care for those who have entered life's most difficult stages."*

Medicinal Murder: Charting the Steady Expansion of Euthanasia in Europe

Wesley J. Smith

In the following viewpoint, Wesley J. Smith argues that the growing acceptance of assisted suicide and euthanasia in Europe shows the moral danger in allowing such practices. Smith claims that legalized euthanasia leads to cultural desensitization to the value of life and a corruption of medical ethics. Smith is a senior fellow at the Discovery Institute's Human Exceptionalism program, a consultant to the Patients Rights Council, and a special consultant for the Center for Bioethics and Culture. He is the author of Forced Exit: Euthanasia, Assisted Suicide and the New Duty to Die.

Wesley J. Smith, "Medicinal Murder: Charting the Steady Expansion of Euthanasia in Europe," *First Things*, no. 233, May 2013, pp. 39–44. Copyright © 2013 by First Things. All rights reserved. Reproduced by permission.

As you read, consider the following questions:

1. In what country was a sexually abused anorexic woman allowed to be euthanized by her psychiatrist, according to Smith?

2. According to the author, thirteen patients with mental illness were euthanized in 2011 in what country?

3. In 2011, the two primary assisted-suicide facilities of what country helped 560 people kill themselves?

The forty-five-year-old twin brothers had not contracted a terminal illness. Nor were Marc and Eddy Verbessem in physical pain. Both had been born deaf and were progressively losing their eyesight. As the *Telegraph* reported, "The pair told doctors that they were unable to bear the thought of not being able to see each other again," and so wanted to die.

When their own doctor wouldn't kill them, they found their executioner in Dr. David Dufour, who told a television newscast: "They had a cup of coffee in the hall, it went well and [they had] a rich conversation. Then the separation from their parents and brother was very serene and beautiful. At the last there was a little wave of their hands and then they were gone."

In a morally sane society, Dufour would lose his license to practice medicine and be tried for homicide. But having legalized euthanasia, Belgium no longer fits that description. The twins were not the first joint euthanasia killings reported in the country. In 2011, Belgian media extolled the joint deaths of an elderly couple, who were lethally injected with the apparent knowledge and support of their local community. They even made their final arrangements at the local mortuary before submitting to their terminations.

The couple's demise was celebrated by a Belgian bioethicist, who said, "It is an important signal to break a taboo." He added in terms as calm and chilling as those of the doctor who killed the twins, "This can be viewed as a normal way of dying and viewed as such by the community at large. . . . Non-terminal partners, as we call them, also have the option of dying together. It is legally possible. There are no legal difficulties. It is only less well known. People think that euthanasia can only be applied to terminal cancer patients. But the group is a lot bigger. And this is a beautiful example that allows us to provide a dignified death to this couple, thanks to euthanasia." Most societies see joint suicides by elderly couples as tragic. For some in Belgium, they are beautiful.

In a separate case early this year, a Belgian psychiatrist euthanized Ann G., a forty-four-year-old woman with severe anorexia who had only a few months earlier publicly accused her previous psychiatrist of persuading her into sexual relations. *Bio-Edge*, an Australian blog that serves as an international clearinghouse for stories involving bioethics, reported that as early as 2007 Ann G. had told a journalist of her wish to commit suicide. Several months before her death, she appeared on a TV program and alleged that her former psychiatrist had sexually abused her and other patients. (The psychiatrist later admitted his guilt.) "Going public," *Bio-Edge* reported, "gave Ann a brief respite from 'the cancer in her head.' However, she was bitterly disappointed that the man who had victimised her was not severely disciplined. Then, overseen by a new psychiatrist, she exercised her option."

The news gets much worse in Belgium. Currently, the government is agitating to allow *minors* to consent to euthanasia if, as the ruling Socialist Party leader Thierry Giet advocates, the child is "capable of discernment or affected by an incurable illness or suffering that we cannot alleviate." Alzheimer's patients will also soon be allowed to consent to euthanasia.

And that isn't the worst of it. In my first published article against euthanasia—"The Whispers of Strangers," published in *Newsweek* in June 1993—I worried that if assisted suicide were ever normalized, one day "organ harvesting" could be added to euthanasia "as a plum to society." In Belgium it now has.

The joining of voluntary euthanasia and organ harvesting came to light in a 2008 letter published in the medical journal *Transplant International*, reporting that a totally paralyzed woman first asked for euthanasia—permission granted—and then asked to donate her organs after her heart stopped. These procedures were deemed ethical simply because they had been performed. "This case of two separate requests . . . demonstrates that organ harvesting after euthanasia may be considered and accepted from ethical, legal, and practical viewpoints" in countries where euthanasia is legal, doctors claim in the letter. Moreover, "this possibility may increase the number of transplantable organs and may also provide some comfort to the donor and his (her) family."

Since this first case, other killings followed by organ harvesting have been reported—including at least one case involving a patient with a severe mental illness. As reported in *Applied Cardiopulmonary Pathophysiology* in 2011, four patients (three disabled and one mentally ill) were euthanized and their lungs harvested. The authors seem to hope for more opportunities to study the efficiency and efficacy of harvesting organs from euthanized patients. "Euthanasia donors accounted for 2.8% of all donors and 23.5% of all DCD [donors after cardiac death]," they noted in their conclusion. Lungs taken from these donors "resulted in excellent immediate graft function and good early outcome comparable to other DCD."

They did worry that one lung condition called BOS (bronchiolitis obliterans syndrome) needed to be studied for its effect on the long-term survival of those who received the lungs. The reason is chilling. "A difference may be expected as the quality of the pulmonary graft from a euthanasia donor may be superior compared to any other brain-dead and cardiac-dead donor," the authors observed. "In contrast to these donors, euthanasia donors do not experience an agonal phase before circulatory arrest as seen in donors dying from hypoxemia or from cardiogenic or hypovolemic shock" and other effects that lead to lung inflammation and thus to neurogenic edema that is "a known risk factor for later development of BOS." That is not the only problem, though. They add that, "on the other hand, a possible toxic effect on human lung tissue of a lethal dose of barbiturates given at the time of euthanasia is not yet known."

Physicians in favor of post-euthanasia organ harvesting have become so emboldened in the seeming acceptance of their agenda that they hold symposia proselytizing for the program to be expanded wherever euthanasia is legal. These symposia specifically target patients with neuromuscular disabilities as best suited to the joint procedure since, unlike cancer patients, they provide "good organs" when they die.

By joining euthanasia with organ donation, Belgium crossed a very dangerous bridge: The country gave society the chance to benefit from mercy killing. But the acceptance of joint killing and harvesting sends a cruel message to disabled and mentally ill people that their deaths could have greater value than their lives. Bromides about "choice" and the voluntary nature of "the process" are mere rationalization.

In the Netherlands, euthanasia was decriminalized in certain cases after a 1973 court ruling that a doctor who followed protective guidelines would not be prosecuted. The doctor could euthanize his patient only if unbearable suffering could be alleviated in no other way, the patient had made repeated requests for euthanasia, a second doctor had confirmed the opinion of the first, and the doctor reported the euthanasia to the coroner. This system continued until 2002, when lethally injecting or assisting the suicides of qualified patients was formally legalized.

From its supposedly restricted and limited beginnings, since 1973 the practice of physician-administered death to those who ask for it has steadily expanded—from the terminally ill, to more seriously chronically ill, to people with serious disabilities, to those suffering from existential anguish or mental illness. Euthanizing the profoundly depressed became legal after the Dutch Supreme Court ruled that a psychiatrist did not break the law when he assisted in the suicide of a chronically grieving patient who wanted to die so she could be buried between her two dead children.

Abuses of the system have been repeatedly reported, with the offenders facing few or no legal or professional consequences when they violate legal guidelines. For example, doctors sometimes euthanize patients who have not asked to die, a practice known as "termination without request or consent." Such cases are rarely prosecuted or meaningfully punished, with a few weeks' suspended sentence a typical sanction in the rare convictions. Infanticide is a regular practice in some Dutch hospitals. The *Lancet* twice reported that about 8 percent of all infants who die in the Netherlands each year— perhaps eighty to ninety cases—are euthanized. Another study found a similar infanticide rate in Flanders, Belgium.

Infanticide remains against the law in the Netherlands, and euthanizing babies is technically murder. But, as in cases of non-voluntary euthanasia, few doctors are prosecuted for euthanizing babies, and, as far as I know, none of those convicted has ever faced professional discipline or anything more than a brief suspended sentence. In fact, infanticide became so acceptable that in 2004, a pediatrics professor at the University Medical Center Groningen published a bureaucratic checklist designed to help doctors determine which terminally ill or severely disabled infants could be euthanized ethically. The Groningen Protocol, as it is known, was ratified by the Dutch national association of pediatricians and even published respectfully in the *New England Journal of Medicine*.

Dutch law enforcement and society are utterly indifferent to these legal violations. The legal guidelines supposedly restricting the practice of euthanasia are ignored with general impunity. Indeed, one can reasonably say the guidelines exist more to give the appearance of control than to provide meaningful preventive barriers.

But these facts are old news. More recent events demonstrate that the practice of euthanasia has grown ever more radical. For example, euthanasia inflicted upon the mentally ill has recently become far more common. A 2012 *Dutch News* story reported that thirteen patients with mental illness had been euthanized in 2011, along with forty-nine patients with early dementia.

Dutch euthanasia authorities explicitly approve such cases through oversight boards called regional committees that review and discuss cases of euthanasia that test the boundaries. For example, the euthanasia death of a woman hospitalized for severe depression was specifically approved in the regional committee's annual report of 2010. She had suffered intermittently from depression since 1980, and since 2005 she had spent most of her time in the hospital. When a final round of treatment failed, the committee held that her mental suffering constituted suitable grounds to be killed. Though she was lucid, she used a wheelchair, had a poor appetite, and slept badly.

The committee report said that "her thinking was not abnormal, nor did she have serious cognitive problems" and that "her mood was depressive, but not psychotic." The patient

> was emotionally unstable, crying all the time and constantly talking about how miserable she felt and how empty, hopeless and unbearable her life was. She had had enough of phasing in new medication and then phasing it out again. She no longer enjoyed anything, she had no energy or feelings left and she had not laughed for four years. She had considered suicide, but did not know how to go about it. She stated that she could no longer cope with reality, since she no longer felt part of it.

Since her suffering "was unbearable, with no prospect of improvement," the committee decided that the doctor "had acted in accordance with the statutory due care criteria."

The same paradigm exists now in the Netherlands for euthanizing the elderly because they are "tired of life" or for non-life-threatening conditions, even existential suffering. Thus, the 2010 report quoted above also approved the euthanasia of an elderly woman who was losing her eyesight and experiencing other typical effects of aging. The woman, who was in her eighties, "could no longer do the things that made life worthwhile to her," such as "reading, philosophising, debating, politics, art and so on." The report explained that she "had always been very independent and had considered this her greatest asset" but was deteriorating physically.

The doctors had talked with her about withholding food and fluids, but the patient thought the period of dependence this would require of her "the most dreadful thing that could happen to her, and she rejected this alternative. She considered it a blessing that she could end her life with the help of euthanasia and would not have to become dependent. The unbearable nature of her suffering was due to her loss of the ability to live a meaningful life."

Certainly, everyone will empathize with the distress a once-vigorous person feels as she experiences debilitation. But often this kind of depression is treatable with proper geriatric psychiatric interventions. Yet there was no indication in the report that psychiatric treatment was even attempted. Despite this, the committee approved the woman's euthanasia as "in accordance with the statutory due care criteria."

In a better world, mental health professionals would push back against killing those suffering existential anguish or certified mental illnesses, no matter how severe. But the Dutch psychiatric journal *Tijdschrift voor Psychiatrie* took the opposite tack, instead celebrating changes that have made it safe for psychiatrists to become a "midwife of death" for their patients and calling euthanasia "an emancipation of the psychiatric patient and psychiatry itself."

According to the article, psychiatrists would be wrong to refuse to kill a patient merely based on personal beliefs: "Categorical rejection of help [to die] in psychiatry represents a failure [to respect] the autonomy of psychiatric patients." And so the last line of defense against the suicides of mentally ill and deeply depressed people—a dedicated mental health professional fighting for the life of every patient—has surrendered to the euthanasia imperative.

The Royal Dutch Medical Association (KNMG) also has condemned doctors who refuse to euthanize legally qualified patients because they have conscientious objections. The KNMG's position paper "The Role of the Physician in the Voluntary Termination of Life," published in 2011, admits that "most physicians find it difficult to perform euthanasia or assisted suicide," but still insists that a doctor who "is not prepared to consider a euthanasia request from patients . . . must then put the patient in touch with a colleague who does not have fundamental objections to euthanasia and assisted suicide. If a physician cannot or does not wish to honor a patient's request for euthanasia or assisted suicide he must give the patient a timely and clear explanation of why, and furthermore must then refer or transfer the patient to another physician in good time."

Though the doctor has "no legal obligation to refer patients, there is a moral and professional duty" to help patients find a doctor who will help them die. In other words, the KNMG holds that every Dutch physician is ethically required to be complicit in legal euthanasia, either by doing the deed or referring to a colleague willing to kill.

The same paper explains that when patients do not qualify for euthanasia, a doctor may legally refer them to how-to-commit-suicide literature, and then discuss the literature with them, in order to help them kill themselves. If the patient decides to deny himself food and water, the doctor must supervise his care and "alleviate the suffering by arranging effective palliative care."

To review: According to the KNMG, it is unprofessional for a doctor to refuse to participate in euthanasia—either by doing the deed or referring so the deed can be done—when a legally qualified patient asks for euthanasia. But it is perfectly acceptable for a physician to teach patients how to commit suicide if they don't qualify for euthanasia under the law. That is an example of why it is called the culture of death.

In the last decade, Switzerland has become Jack Kevorkian as a country. During the 1990s, about 130 disabled, depressed, and/or terminally ill people traveled from all over the United States to Kevorkian's home state of Michigan to commit suicide with his help. (The suicide trips ended when the doctor was imprisoned in 2000 for murder after videotaping himself lethally injecting a man suffering from Lou Gehrig's disease and taking it to *60 Minutes* for broadcasting.) But now, Kevorkianism is back in the form of "suicide tourism," the flow of people traveling to Switzerland to be killed at the country's legal suicide clinics.

Assisted suicide was legalized in Switzerland in 1942. Unlike the situation in the Netherlands and Belgium, in Switzerland *anyone* can participate as long the reason for helping is not a "selfish motive." For decades, the Swiss law made barely a ripple. But then, with the emergence of an international euthanasia movement, enterprising ideologues opened new facilities, creating a growth industry. In 2011 the nation's two primary assisted-suicide facilities helped a staggering 560 people to kill themselves (up from 350 in 2006). That's nearly two suicides each day.

Swiss suicide clinics do not restrict their services to the terminally ill. Many of their customers are disabled or depressed. For example, the parents of Daniel James made headlines when they flew their son from the United Kingdom to Switzerland to commit suicide after he was paralyzed from injuries sustained while playing rugby.

There have also been joint suicides in Swiss clinics, most notably the famous English conductor Sir Edward Downes and his wife Joan, who flew together to Switzerland to die at the assisted-suicide facility run by the advocacy group Dignitas—a decision endorsed in the media by their children. (Joan had been diagnosed with cancer, and Sir Edward was almost blind.)

Dignitas was also instrumental in bringing a case to the Swiss Supreme Court to legalize assisted suicide for the mentally ill. The court complied, ruling, "It must be recognized that an incurable, permanent, serious mental disorder can cause similar suffering as a physical disorder, making life unbearable to the patient in the long term." Once the ideological premises of assisted suicide are accepted, ultimately there is no way to stop its expansion.

Swiss law does not permit actual euthanasia, that is, when the lethal act is performed by someone other than the person who dies. But that soon may change, thanks to a court ruling that refused to penalize a doctor who inserted a lethal drip into a paralyzed patient's vein. According to media reports about the case, the court ruled that since the patient wished to die, "the doctor in this case had a medical and moral duty to break the law."

Advocacy groups have wielded suicide tourism as a cudgel to shatter the public's resistance to legalizing assisted suicide—just as the line of people flying to Michigan in the 1990s helped to soften up America. England has been particularly targeted for the argument that people should be able to kill themselves at home, surrounded by family, rather than having to fly to Switzerland to do it. Polling shows that this argument resonates with many Europeans, indicating that at least some people now view suicide as a *necessity* in circumstances involving serious illness or disability.

The English media have energetically exploited tourism suicides in the same way the American media did deaths facilitated by Kevorkian. Just as in 1998, when *60 Minutes* played Kevorkian's video of his murder of Thomas Youk, the BBC aired a video of an assisted suicide that took place in a Swiss clinic—complete with narration by a famous euthanasia advocate.

Airing the actual suicide violated World Health Organization media guidelines. As the WHO's "Preventing Suicide: A Resource for Media Professionals" states: "Television . . . influences suicidal behavior. [One study] showed an increase in suicide up to ten days after television news reports of cases of suicide. As in the printed media, highly publicized stories that appear in multiple programs on multiple channels seem to carry the greatest impact—all the more so if they involve celebrities." To prevent one suicide from leading to others, the WHO instructs the media to avoid glorifying or sensationalizing suicide, publishing photographs or suicide notes, and reporting details on the methods used.

Thus the BBC did precisely what it isn't supposed to according to suicide prevention guidelines. I don't think there is much doubt that media sensationalism in England has both promoted suicide tourism and concomitantly boosted the potency of assisted-suicide advocacy there—which is probably the point.

What conclusions can we draw from the European euthanasia experience that might be of use in the United States as we grapple with these issues? First, once assisted suicide or euthanasia is legalized, it will not long remain a limited enterprise. This is not a "slippery slope" alarmist projection but a conclusion abundantly demonstrated by facts on the ground in Belgium, the Netherlands, and Switzerland. There is no gain-saying that once euthanasia gains widespread public and medical professional support, the supposedly strict guidelines designed to prevent "abuses" become, at most, low hurdles easily circumvented or ignored.

Second, legalizing euthanasia changes culture. Not only do the categories of people eligible for euthanasia expand, but the rest of society generally ceases to think that it matters. This desensitizing, in turn, affects how people perceive the moral value of the seriously ill, disabled, and elderly—and perhaps how they view themselves.

Third, euthanasia corrupts medical ethics by mutating the role of doctors into purveyors of death rather than consistent enablers of life. The hospice movement seeks to improve life by maximizing the patient's health, comfort, and inclusion in the human community until his natural death. In contrast, euthanasia intentionally cuts short the patient's life through lethal means. To put it another way, hospice is about living, euthanasia is about dying.

Fourth, once a person is deemed the member of a killable caste, it becomes easier to reduce his worth to that of a mere natural resource that can be exploited for the benefit of society.

Finally, I think widespread popular acceptance of euthanasia in Europe—recent polls show strong support, including in relatively conservative countries like Poland—is a symptom of cultural nihilism. Consider: A hundred years ago, when people really did die in agony, there was little call for legalizing euthanasia. Yet today, when most pain can be significantly alleviated if not eliminated, we see calls for so-called "death with dignity." Clearly, more is going on than just a desire to eliminate suffering.

What is the antidote? Love. We all age. We fall ill. We grow weak. We become disabled. Life can get very hard. Euthanasia raises the fundamental question of whether our culture will retain the moral capacity to sustain a culture of care for those who have entered life's most difficult stages. On that question, it seems to me, hangs the moral future of Western civilization. For as the Canadian journalist Andrew Coyne has cogently warned: "A society that believes in nothing can offer no argument even against death. A culture that has lost its faith in life cannot comprehend why it should be endured."

Periodical and Internet Sources Bibliography

The following articles have been selected to supplement the diverse views presented in this chapter.

Mike Adams	"Poverty, Rape and Abortion," *Townhall*, July 18, 2011.
Andrew Brown	"Assisted Suicide Is Never an Autonomous Choice," *Guardian* (UK), January 5, 2012.
Christopher Caldwell	"The Right to Die Will Put Us on a Very Slippery Slope," *Financial Times* (UK), September 20, 2013.
Colleen Carroll Campbell	"Abortion Proponents Distort the Meaning of Personhood," *St. Louis Post-Dispatch*, August 26, 2010.
Selwyn Duke	"Biden's Abortion Blarney," *American Thinker*, October 15, 2012.
Edmund C. Hurlbutt	"Abortion 'Rights' and the Duty Not to Know," *Human Life Review*, Summer 2011.
Jaime Joyce	"The Evolving State of Physician-Assisted Suicide," *Atlantic*, July 16, 2012.
Kenneth W. Krause	"Abortion's Still Unanswered Questions," *Humanist*, July–August 2011.
Andrew Napolitano	"Is Rape a Moral Justification for Abortion?," Reason.com, August 23, 2012.
Wesley J. Smith	"Preventing (Some) Suicides," *First Things*, February 2014.
Marc A. Thiessen	"Bringing Humanity Back to the Abortion Debate," *Washington Post*, April 19, 2010.
Mary Elizabeth Williams	"So What If Abortion Ends Life?," *Salon*, January 23, 2013.

OPPOSING
VIEWPOINTS®
SERIES

CHAPTER 3

Should Religious Beliefs About Ethics Justify Behavior?

Chapter Preface

Although ethics and law sometimes overlap, not all behavior that may be considered ethical is legally mandated. Conversely, some would argue that certain laws we have are unethical; in the United States, this is a frequent charge against legal abortion. Following the law is a requirement of each citizen in the United States, but the First Amendment to the US Constitution provides for the "free exercise of religion," and sometimes religious values come into conflict with existing laws.

In certain cases, American society has provided exceptions to certain laws or rules by people who have ethical objections. A prime example of this is the conscientious objection exception in the US military. Since the Civil War, there has been a history of exempting from military service those who object to war on religious grounds. The 1940 Selective Training and Service Act noted that exemption must be based on "religious training and belief," and in 1948 Congress specified that this was defined as "an individual's belief in a relation to a Supreme Being involving duties superior to those arising from any human relation" and did not include beliefs that were "essentially political, sociological, or philosophical views or a merely personal moral code." However, a US Supreme Court decision in 1965 found that "religious" could encompass moral or ethical beliefs that have the same strength of traditional religious convictions. This exemption was particularly relevant during times of mandatory conscription but is less so today with voluntary military service. Nonetheless, this kind of exception to the general laws is notable in allowing religious views—as well as personal moral views—to exempt one from the laws that apply to everyone else.

Exemptions to military service are not the only exemptions to laws made in the case of deeply held moral or religious beliefs. Most states and localities offer parents the option of exempting their children from school vaccination requirements for religious reasons, and many allow exemptions for philosophical or ethical reasons.

The federal Religious Freedom Restoration Act of 1993 established that when individuals object to laws on religious grounds, they must be granted an exemption unless the government can show a compelling reason in denying them the exemption. Most states have similar protections. Thus, for example, a religious person who believed in child sacrifice as a part of her religion would likely not be granted an exemption from homicide laws because of the compelling state interests in protecting innocent people. In less extreme cases, however, it remains unclear how far society is willing to go to allow some people exemptions from the laws based on values they hold as religious people. The viewpoints in this chapter debate whether religious beliefs about ethics should justify behavior.

| *"Religious professionals have the right to pursue a livelihood, and that right is seriously compromised by a society that instinctively dismisses their concerns."* |

Conscience Objections Based on Religion and Morals Must Be Allowed

Kathleen Hunker

In the following viewpoint, Kathleen Hunker argues that individuals should have the right to abstain from professional or business activities that conflict with the ethical values they hold as religious people. Hunker contends that it is unjust to ask religious people to avoid all professions where such a conflict might occur, since that would result in being excluded from the market. Hunker is a policy analyst with the Center for Economic Freedom at the Texas Public Policy Foundation.

As you read, consider the following questions:

1. According to Hunker, what is the idea behind the common reflex to disregard the professional concerns of religious people?

2. If Christians were to avoid occupations that might lead to conflict with their beliefs, Hunker claims which occupations would be closed to them?

3. Hunker contends that disregarding the hardships of religious professionals and excluding them from the market violates the nation's commitment to what two principles?

Just before Christmas [2011], a New Jersey hospital finally agreed that it will no longer force its nurses to assist with any abortion-related services. The settlement concluded an emotional battle between the hospital's administration and 12 pro-life nurses, who objected to the procedures on religious and moral grounds.

The Concerns of Religious People

The New Jersey controversy prompted a series of questions regarding the rights of individuals who oppose abortion, and whether they retain the right to abstain from facilitating what they view as the termination of a human life in the course of their professional and/or business activities. How far does the individual right of conscience extend in light of some states' expressed interest in offering cost-effective abortion services? It is a valid and disputed question.

Of course, this unresolved tension between religious liberty and changing social policy exists beyond the contours of a university hospital. These questions surface routinely over a wide range of issues and in a wide range of professions. In the 1990s, the government inquired whether practicing Christians could decline renting to cohabitating heterosexual couples. Hospitality companies question whether they can opt out of hosting same-sex "marriage" celebrations, and then there is the vigorously contested matter of pharmacies refusing to dispense contraception.

A common reflex is to disregard the concerns of religious professionals because we view them as self-inflicted. After all, as the sentiment goes, if you have an objection to dispensing certain medications, do not become a pharmacist.

I would be more satisfied with this response if it were limited to a single profession, but that is not the case. A single religious belief can raise questions of conscience in an anthology of unrelated vocations, and an entire catechism of religious beliefs can exclude the faithful from the market in its entirety. As a consequence, if society gives conscience rights no regard whatsoever, religious individuals could find themselves effectively excluded from pursuing a livelihood.

Moral Beliefs in the Marketplace

To demonstrate how this works, I compiled a non-exhaustive list of occupations "closed off" to practicing Christians under the philosophy that those who believe in traditional morality should simply avoid particular professions. Each example listed comes from a recent legal action that made this very claim.

According to the philosophy I detailed, practicing Christians cannot operate a catering hall, practice psychology, run a hotel, work as an independent photographer, launch a video-duplication company, rent out apartments (even if it is in their own home), teach in public schools, work as a guidance counselor, run for a clerk's office, manage a restaurant, open up a florist, oversee and operate an adoption agency, become a social worker, become a pharmacist, start a fertility clinic, serve as a doctor or nurse, or even practice law.

Without conscience protections, Christians find themselves barred from each listed profession—all because of their commitment to a single Christian belief. And let us be frank: religions consist of more than one individual tenet. If you were to consider the breadth of the entire Christian faith, which includes other potentially controversial positions, you would ex-

---

Support for Health Care Conscience Rights

*77% of American adults surveyed said it is either "very" or "somewhat" important to them "that healthcare professionals in the U.S. are **not forced to participate** in procedures or practices to which they have **moral objections." 16%** said it is not important.*

Total **important** (net)	77%
Very important	52%
Somewhat important	25%
Total **not important** (net)	16%
Not too important	8%
Not at all important	8%
Do not know/depends	8%
Refused	1%

TAKEN FROM: The Polling Company Inc., Phone Survey of the American Public, April 29–May 1, 2011.

---

pand that list to the point where traditional Christians could not enter the marketplace without being forced to choose between a secure livelihood and the state of their soul. The same is true of all religious faiths.

Excluding Christians from service professions not only impacts the professionals—it takes choices away from patients, who often want to choose a counselor or doctor who shares their core values. . . .

The Importance of Conscience Protections

Imposing one set of values on all professionals vastly reduces the choices available in a diverse marketplace. Society, therefore, needs conscience protections in order to ensure that religious individuals can participate in the market as both entrepreneurs and consumers.

Disregarding the hardships of religious professionals as avoidable and self-inflicted leads to the near exclusion of religious individuals from the public market. Such a scenario seems irreconcilable with our nation's commitment to diversity and liberty.

We live in a society of competing and contradictory beliefs. If we are to stay true to our national promise of equal liberty to all, then we cannot exclude entire populations from the marketplace simply because we disagree with their values or fail to share their hardship. Conscience protections provide some give in the joints of society; they enable people of conflicting beliefs to live with one another.

Religious professionals have the right to pursue a livelihood, and that right is seriously compromised by a society that instinctively dismisses their concerns. A diverse society requires compromise in order to be successful. As such, the conscience rights of individuals should be defended whenever possible.

"A pluralistic society cannot simply accept blanket exemptions from duly enacted laws because would-be lawbreakers claim religious sanction."

Bakers of Conscience

Ed Kilgore

*In the following viewpoint, Ed Kilgore argues that exemptions to
laws based on religious values are problematic. Nonetheless,
Kilgore notes that there is a history in the United States of ac-
commodating religious objections with legal exceptions, making
the new requests for exemptions difficult to wave away. Kilgore
claims that many of the new claims, however, are suspect. Kilgore
is a contributing writer to the* Washington Monthly, *managing
editor for the* Democratic Strategist, *and a senior fellow at the*
Progressive Policy Institute.

As you read, consider the following questions:

1. What question is at the center of the dispute over religious liberty interests involved in enforcing nondiscrimination laws, according to Kilgore?

2. What three examples does the author provide of past
   concessions given to religious people exempting them
   from certain laws?

3. What does Kilgore suggest that bakers who object to
same-sex marriage do to avoid conflict with their religion?

At the end of a solid piece by MoJo's Dana Liebelson on
the coordinated nature of the sudden effusion of "religious liberty" legislation being introduced in Republican-controlled states, there is an interesting quote from gay rights
advocate Evan Hurst:

> "This seems to be a concerted Hail Mary campaign to carve
> out special rights for religious conservatives so that they
> don't have to play by the same rules as everyone else does,"
> says Hurst, from Truth Wins Out. "In this new up-is-down
> world, anti-gay religious folks are 'practicing their faith'
> when they're baking cakes or renting out hotel rooms to
> travelers. On the ground, [these bills] hurt real, live LGBT
> people."

The question of what constitutes "practicing faith" is at the
center of a lot of the dispute over the alleged "religious liberty" (and hence First Amendment) interests involved in enforcing nondiscrimination laws (or for that matter, laws making it legal to purchase contraceptives or offer abortion
services).

It is not, I would submit, necessarily an easy question, either. Yes, the common conservative argument that anything
other than a blanket exemption for "faith-based" civil disobedience—and a deference to religious arguments in debates
over entirely secular topics—means constricting believers to
catacombs where they tremble in fear is ludicrous. Nobody is
talking about suppressing conservative speech, no matter how
obnoxious and (in my view at least) un-Christian. And vaguely
alluding to "the public square" as a place for religious expression doesn't mean much either, other than that those monotonously using this phrase have been exposed at some point to
the vast influence of Richard John Neuhaus, who himself of-

ten seemed to view the very existence of religiously offensive laws and habits to represent persecution or at least excuse revolutionary defiance of the secular "regime."

But unless we are prepared to rescind past concessions to the Amish over mandatory school attendance laws, or to Christian pacifists over the draft, or to Jehovah's Witnesses over oath-taking—just to cite a few major examples—it's not enough either to just wave away any religiously based claims for special treatment as laughable or as offensive to American traditions.

In turn, though, these precedents all involved long periods of negotiation between secular and religious authorities to carve out exceptions and authenticate those who took advantage of them. No state passed laws exempting anyone who claimed a religious objection to school attendance laws to yank the kids out of school, no questions asked. In all cases, those claiming exemptions had to establish, via religious authorities, that the laws in question threatened the viability of their communities (viz. the Amish) or required them to commit grievous sins (viz. "conscientious objectors" to participation in the military).

The legitimacy of such claims aren't always that clear from the religious as well as the secular perspective; that's why there was such a large and inconclusive conflict in the early Christian church over consumption of meat sacrificed in pagan rituals.

I suppose the famous "pharmacists of conscience" who refuse to dispense what they consider "abortifacients," and who also believe abortion is homicide in the biblical sense, have a plausible argument that they are being forced to violate their consciences on a matter of grave moral importance, though they aren't the ones committing the sins. But those who refuse to sell a properly prescribed oral contraceptive to a teenager because they frown on their "immoral" behavior? They are at most passive and essentially meaningless interme-

The Problem with Conscience Exemptions

What's really wrong with conscience clauses? We all have consciences, and laws that exist to protect us from being forced to violate our religious and ethical principles should be welcome on the left and right. The problem isn't conscience clause legislation so much as what we might call conscience creep: a slow but systematic effort to use religious conscience claims to sidestep laws that should apply to everyone.

Dahlia Lithwick, "Conscience Creep:
What's So Wrong with Conscience Clauses?,"
Slate, October 3, 2013.

diaries in the supposed transgressions of doctors and patients, not to mention meddling busybodies.

But it's a bit of a stretch to talk of "bakers of conscience" or "travel agents of conscience." Are civil laws regarding marriage so central to religious faith that acknowledging the fact that a same-sex marriage is legal somehow makes the baker or the wedding planner or the travel agent complicit in "evil?" Not unless (a) you are part of a faith community (e.g., High Calvinists) that holds obedience to God requires striving for everyone's obedience to God; or (b) you subscribe to the increasingly ludicrous idea that same-sex marriage will "destroy" heterosexual marriage through some bizarre process of disrespect.

I'm sure I'm not the only one who suspects the baker who doesn't want to put two men on the wedding cake is motivated by an "ick factor" of simple bigotry rather than any agonized crisis of conscience or faith. And I'm not at all reluctant to say that bakers who do feel that way might want to avoid the near occasion of sin by going into a different line of work, just as a pacifist probably should not enter the armed forces even if the odds of being in combat are low.

But a pluralistic society cannot simply accept blanket exemptions from duly enacted laws because would-be lawbreakers claim religious sanction. And refusing them is hardly an act of regression, and certainly don't force religious people to cower in their homes and churches.

> "Americans do not forfeit their right to live and work in accordance with their faith simply because they go into business."

Employers Should Not Be Forced to Provide for Objectionable Health Care

Elizabeth H. Slattery and Sarah Torre

In the following viewpoint, Elizabeth H. Slattery and Sarah Torre argue that the federal requirement that employers pay for coverage of health care insurance that covers care that conflicts with their religious beliefs violates their First Amendment right to religious freedom. The authors contend that the US Supreme Court should reject this anti-conscience mandate. Slattery is a senior legal policy analyst in the Heritage Foundation's Edwin Meese III Center for Legal and Judicial Studies. Torre is a policy analyst in the foundation's DeVos Center for Religion and Civil Society.

Elizabeth H. Slattery and Sarah Torre, "Obamacare Anti-Conscience Mandate at the Supreme Court," Legal Memorandum #115, The Heritage Foundation, February 13, 2014, pp. 1–7. All rights reserved. Copyright © 2014 by The Heritage Foundation. Reproduced by permission.

As you read, consider the following questions:

1. According to the authors, what is the fine for non-exempted employers who fail to provide health insurance?

2. What is the main issue before the US Supreme Court in the cases the authors discuss?

3. According to the authors, what health care coverage does the Korte family claim is in violation of religious values?

In February 2012, the U.S. Department of Health and Human Services (HHS) finalized guidelines requiring employers to pay for coverage of contraception, sterilization, and abortion-inducing drugs and granted a narrow exemption for certain religious employers. Many employers believe that complying with this mandate would violate the tenets of their faith, but failure to adhere to the law could result in steep fines—in the case of one company, an estimated $1.3 million per day.

In an effort to block the anti-conscience mandate, religious organizations and other private employers have filed over 90 lawsuits with more than 300 plaintiffs. The Supreme Court of the United States has agreed to review two of the for-profit cases later in the 2013–2014 term. The court will consider two questions:

- Does the mandate violate the First Amendment guarantee of the free exercise of religion?

- Who can exercise religion under the Religious Freedom Restoration Act?

The Anti-Conscience Mandate

In March 2010, Congress passed the Patient Protection and Affordable Care Act, better known as Obamacare, which forces employers to offer health insurance and expands the federal standards for what those health plans must cover. Those benefit standards, the details of which are largely left to the discretion of the administration, include new mandates on preventive services that must be covered in qualified insurance policies and employee health plans without imposing any cost-sharing (deductibles or co-payments) on the insured individuals. Non-exempted employers, secular or religious, are required to offer coverage that includes the services mandated under the health care law—or face significant federal fines.

In July 2010, the Department of Health and Human Services published an interim final rule implementing the preventive services mandate. That interim rulemaking noted that the Health Resources and Services Administration (HRSA) would later identify, per the statutory instructions, additional mandated preventive services specifically for women.

In August 2011, HHS amended the interim final rule to include the HRSA "guidelines" for women's preventive services, one of which is "[a]ll Food and Drug Administration approved contraceptive methods, sterilization procedures, and patient education and counseling for all women with reproductive capacity." Those methods include drugs such as Plan B and ella and some intrauterine devices, which can cause an abortion very early in pregnancy. Many religious organizations, family businesses, and other employers have deeply held moral or religious objections to such life-ending drugs or contraception, yet the same HRSA guidelines also included a very narrow religious exemption that effectively applied only to formal houses of worship.

In February 2012, the [Barack] Obama administration finalized the preventive services mandate rulemaking, including the HRSA guidelines that all qualified health plans must include coverage of abortion-inducing drugs and devices, contraception, and sterilization. As of August 1, 2012, at the renewal of the employers' health plans, all private, for-profit employers offering qualified health care coverage were mandated to include these drugs, devices, and services in their health plans without any enrollee cost-sharing requirement.

Offering an employee health plan that does not include these mandated items can result in a fine of up to $100 per enrollee per day. Employers can choose to avoid the fine by dropping health care coverage altogether, but such a choice would not be without financial consequences. Under Obamacare, non-exempted employers with 50 or more full-time employees that do not provide health insurance will be forced to pay a fine of roughly $2,000 per year for each full-time employee beyond the first 30 workers who is not offered a health plan.

An Amendment to the Mandate

Although the Obama administration amended the original religious exemption to the mandate on July 2, 2013, the final exemption extends only to formal houses of worship and their integrated auxiliaries, such as church-run soup kitchens. All other religious employers—hospitals, schools, social service organizations, and the like—and all for-profit businesses must comply with the mandate or risk burdensome fines.

Under the final rule, nonprofit religious organizations that are not already exempt may self-certify to a third-party administrator for an "accommodation," which supposedly allows employers to avoid directly paying for or providing health insurance coverage that violates their beliefs. However, along with the self-certification, the organization would have to provide a complete list (with identifying information) of the employees and dependents covered by its plan, thereby requiring the organization to initiate and facilitate the process of the third-party administrator's obtaining coverage for the contraceptive products, abortion-inducing drugs, services, and counseling for those individuals.

This accommodation is in effect a shell game, as a district court recognized when it granted preliminary relief in a recent challenge. The court held that although this accommodation would enable the plaintiffs to avoid directly paying for those portions of the health plan to which they object, it would merely shift the responsibility for purchasing such coverage to a secular source, which would "not absolve or exonerate them from the moral turpitude created by the 'accommodation.'"

The First Amendment and the Religious Freedom Restoration Act

The First Amendment states that "Congress shall make no law respecting an establishment of religion, or prohibiting the free exercise thereof. . . ." The Supreme Court of the United States has held that the government may not require an individual to choose between complying with the tenets of his faith or the law. For example:

- In *West Virginia State Board of Education v. Barnette*, the Supreme Court ruled in favor of school-age Jehovah's Witnesses who, for religious reasons, objected to being forced to recite the Pledge of Allegiance and salute the American flag;

- In *Sherbert v. Verner*, the court declared that a state may not deny unemployment benefits to an individual because her faith prohibited her from working on Saturdays; and

- In *Wisconsin v. Yoder*, the court determined that a state may not force Amish parents to send their teenage children to high school against their religious convictions.

The court has repeatedly recognized that if there is a "fixed star in our constitutional constellation, it is that no official . . . can prescribe what shall be orthodox in politics, nationalism, religion, or other matters of opinion."

The court has held, however, that a generally applicable criminal statute prohibiting the use of peyote did not violate the free exercise rights of individuals who use peyote for sacramental purposes. In response to that decision, Congress passed the Religious Freedom Restoration Act (RFRA) to strengthen First Amendment protections—even against generally applicable laws. RFRA prohibits the federal government from "substantially burden[ing] a person's exercise of religion even if the burden results from a rule of general applicability" except where the government shows that the burden "is in furtherance of a compelling governmental interest; and [] is the least restrictive means of furthering that . . . interest." RFRA broadly defines "religious exercise" as "any exercise of religion, whether or not compelled by, or central to, a system of religious belief."

Neither the First Amendment nor RFRA indicates *who* may exercise religion, and the Supreme Court has not directly addressed whether for-profit corporations may do so. The federal appellate courts have grappled with this question in deciding whether to allow for-profit corporate challenges against the anti-conscience mandate to proceed. As these challenges reach the Supreme Court, the main issue before the justices is whether a closely held, family-owned, for-profit corporation can exercise religion.

The Challengers and the Lower Court Decisions

Over 90 suits have been filed challenging the coercive Obamacare mandate as a violation both of the First Amendment's guarantee of the free exercise of religion and of RFRA. Roughly half of the challenges were brought by nonprofit religious organizations, including health care providers, dioceses, schools, and charities; for-profit companies brought the other half. In November 2013, the Supreme Court agreed to review two cases brought by for-profit family businesses.

The federal appellate courts that have issued decisions have reached a range of conclusions: Some have found that the corporation itself cannot exercise religion, while others have concluded that corporations and the families who own and operate them deserve First Amendment protection. Who are the challengers, and how have the appellate courts decided their cases so far?

Conestoga Wood. Conestoga Wood Specialties is a closely held, family-owned corporation in Pennsylvania with 950 employees that manufactures kitchen cabinets. The owners, the Hahns, run Conestoga Wood according to their Mennonite faith, which includes offering an employee health plan aligned with those values. The anti-conscience mandate, however, forces Conestoga Wood to provide and pay for coverage of abortion-inducing drugs and devices—despite the Hahns' religious objections. Conestoga Wood faces fines of up to $95,000 per day for sticking to their deeply held beliefs and not complying with the mandate.

The Hahns sued to enjoin implementation of the mandate, arguing that it violates their free exercise of religion in violation of the First Amendment as well as RFRA. The federal district court denied their motion for a preliminary injunction, finding that a for-profit corporation cannot exercise religion and, further, that the anti-conscience mandate did not substantially burden the Hahns' religious exercise.

The Hahns then appealed to the U.S. Court of Appeals for the Third Circuit, which denied their request for a temporary halt to the mandate. The Third Circuit noted that for-profit businesses are "artificial being[s], invisible, intangible, and existing only in contemplation of law" and could not exercise "an inherently 'human' right" like the free exercise of religion.

The court acknowledged that some businesses may exercise religion: Religious organizations and churches enjoy free exercise protection because they are "means by which individuals practice religion." A for-profit corporation, the court reasoned, could not exercise religion "apart from its owners." However, as a dissenting judge argued, drawing a distinction

The Essence of Religious Freedom

Americans understand intuitively that the essence of religious freedom is that government can't willy-nilly force people to do things that violate their religious beliefs. Some may argue that there's a conflict here between religious freedom and women's rights, but that's a "false choice" (as the president likes to say). Without the HHS [Department of Health and Human Services] rule, women will still be free to obtain contraceptives, abortions, and whatever else isn't illegal. They just won't be able to force their employer to pay for them.

Ilya Shapiro, "Symposium:
Mandates Make Martyrs Out of Corporate Owners,"
SCOTUSblog, *February 24, 2014.*

between businesses based on their "profit motive[s]" flies in the face of reason and, in fact, has been rejected by the Supreme Court in other First Amendment cases.

The court also rejected the notion that a corporation is an "instrument through and by which [the owners] express their religious beliefs," finding instead that the Hahns chose to create an entity with "legally distinct rights and responsibilities." Just as the Hahns' claims may not "pass through" Conestoga Wood, the court concluded, the Hahns' claims based on a legal duty imposed on Conestoga Wood were not likely to succeed.

The Hahns subsequently petitioned the Supreme Court for a writ of certiorari, asking the court to review whether the anti-conscience mandate violates their rights or the rights of their closely held for-profit corporation. The Supreme Court granted this petition for certiorari on November 26, 2013, and will hear oral argument on March 25, 2014.

Hobby Lobby. Hobby Lobby stores and Mardel Christian and Education stores are closely held family businesses headquartered in Oklahoma. Hobby Lobby has grown from a 300-square-foot garage to over 500 arts and craft stores in 41 states and employs more than 13,000 people. Mardel is a chain of 35 Christian bookstores with nearly 400 employees. The owners of both of these businesses, the Green family, are committed not only to serving their customers and employees, but also to investing in communities through partnerships with numerous Christian ministries.

The Greens seek to operate their businesses in accordance with Christian principles, which includes closing all their locations on Sundays and offering an employee health care plan that aligns with their Christian values. They do not wish to provide and pay for coverage of four drugs and devices mandated by the government, and the failure to comply with this mandate could subject Hobby Lobby and Mardel to a total of up to $1.3 million per day ($475 million per year). Alternatively, they could drop the employee health insurance plan and pay a combined fine of $26 million per year.

Hobby Lobby and Mardel challenged the anti-conscience mandate in federal court under RFRA and the free exercise clause and asked for a preliminary injunction to avoid paying the crippling fines while their case is pending. The district court and a two-judge panel of the U.S. Court of Appeals for the Tenth Circuit both denied preliminary relief. Hobby Lobby and Mardel then filed an application for emergency relief with the Supreme Court (considered by Justice Sonia Sotomayor), which also denied relief.

The full Tenth Circuit, however, agreed to reconsider the request for a preliminary injunction and issued a sweeping decision in favor of the plaintiffs. The Tenth Circuit determined that for-profit businesses, just like individuals, can engage in religious exercise because they are "persons" for the purposes of RFRA. Since that statute does not define "person," the court looked to the Dictionary Act, which defines a "person" for purposes of federal law to "include[] corporations . . . as well as individuals."

The court concluded that there was no reason to grant constitutional protection for a business's political expression (as the Supreme Court did in *Citizens United v. Federal Election Commission*) but deny such protection for religious expression. Comparing Hobby Lobby's and Mardel's predicament to that of a kosher butcher forced to follow a law mandating non-kosher butchering practices, the court stated that there was "no reason why one must orient one's business toward a religious community to preserve Free Exercise protections."

Having determined that Hobby Lobby and Mardel may advance these claims, the court found that the anti-conscience mandate imposed a substantial burden on the plaintiffs' exercise of religion under RFRA. Indeed, the court stated that it would be "difficult to characterize the pressure as anything but substantial" since Hobby Lobby and Mardel faced a choice between compromising their beliefs or paying ruinous fines. The court determined that the government's asserted compelling interests for the mandate (public health and gender equality) did not justify the burden placed on Hobby Lobby and Mardel and that the government did not show how granting an exemption to the plaintiffs for four methods of contraception would undermine those interests.

Following the Tenth Circuit's decision, the case returned to the district court, which granted a preliminary injunction. The government asked the Supreme Court to review whether RFRA permits a for-profit corporation to "deny its employees the health coverage of contraceptives to which the employees are otherwise entitled by federal law, based on the religious objections of the corporation's owners." The Supreme Court granted this petition for certiorari and consolidated it with Conestoga. . . .

[Korte & Luitjohan] Contractors and Grote Industries. The Korte family owns an Illinois-based construction company with 90 employees (70 of whom receive health insurance through a union). The Grote family runs an Indiana-based company that manufactures vehicle safety systems. They have more than 1,100 employees worldwide, with about 460 in the United States. Both families seek to operate their companies according to their Roman Catholic faith, so they object to providing and paying for a health insurance plan that covers abortion-inducing drugs and devices, contraception, and sterilization. Their failure to comply with the contraception mandate subjects [Korte & Luitjohan] Contractors to $730,000 and Grote Industries to $17 million per year in fines.

Both families and companies filed suit, alleging violations of RFRA and the free exercise clause, among others, and both were denied preliminary relief by district courts. The U.S. Court of Appeals for the Seventh Circuit temporarily enjoined enforcement of the anti-conscience mandate against these companies pending appeal.

The cases were consolidated, and the Seventh Circuit held that the Kortes and Grotes—as well as their companies—may challenge the mandate. The court reasoned that the owners "have a direct and personal interest in vindicating their individual religious-liberty rights" that is independent from their companies' rights. Like the Tenth Circuit in [the Hobby Lobby case], the court determined that for-profit corporations are "persons" under RFRA and can exercise religion because there is "nothing inherently incompatible between religious exercise and profit-seeking." The court found that the mandate "essentially force[s] the Kortes and Grotes to choose between saving their companies and following the moral teachings of their faith."

Having held that the owners and companies may assert RFRA claims, the court then determined that the anti-conscience mandate substantially burdens their religious exercise. While the government argued that the mandate is too attenuated to constitute a substantial burden on the free exercise of religion, the court pointed out that this "focuses on the wrong thing—the employee's use of contraception—and addresses the wrong question—how many steps separate the employer's act of paying for contraception coverage and an employee's decision to use it." The court maintained that "[n]o civil authority can decide" whether providing the mandated coverage "impermissibly assist[s] the commission of a wrongful act" in violation of church teaching.

The court further highlighted that the government did not make "*any* effort to explain how the contraception mandate is the least restrictive means of furthering its stated goals of promoting public health and gender equality." The court reversed and remanded to the district courts with instructions to enter preliminary injunctions against enforcing the mandate against these companies.

The Right to Exercise Religion

The anti-conscience mandate forces family businesses to provide health insurance plans that cover abortion-inducing drugs and devices, contraception, and sterilization. Many employers believe that complying with this mandate would conflict with the tenets of their faith. Consequently, these employers face the choice of paying steep fines or violating their faith. The First Amendment and the Religious Freedom Restoration Act protect the free exercise of religion, and the many family-run businesses challenging the anti-conscience mandate argue that they deserve protection, too.

The Supreme Court has agreed to review two challenges brought by Hobby Lobby and Conestoga Wood. It will consider whether family-run businesses can exercise religion and, if so, how such a ruling would affect the anti-conscience mandate. Americans do not forfeit their right to live and work in accordance with their faith simply because they go into business to provide for themselves, their families, and their employees.

| "The assumption seems to be that religion releases you from any obligation of any kind to the state."

Religious Freedom Does Not Allow Employer Denial of Health Care

Garrett Epps

In the following viewpoint, Garrett Epps argues that recent requests to be exempt from the contraception mandate in the Patient Protection and Affordable Care Act are not justified by religious objection. Epps contends that the interests at stake in these cases involve not only the employers, but also the interests of the government and the interests of employees. He argues that the legitimate health interests and religious freedom of employees run counter to an employer's interest in opting out of government programs. Epps is a professor of law at the University of Baltimore.

As you read, consider the following questions:

1. According to Epps, what exactly do the Little Sisters object to under the Patient Protection and Affordable Care Act?

2. What religious belief popular many decades ago does Epps give as an example where government would never consider an exemption to the law?

3. What does the author contend is remarkable about the circuit court's opinion about Hobby Lobby's request for exemption?

Lawyers should always listen to what judges say. Believing it, though, is often a mistake.

Take these words: "This order should not be construed as an expression of the Court's views on the merits." It's the last sentence of the court's order, issued Friday [January 24, 2014], in *Little Sisters of the Poor v. Sebelius*, a religious order's challenge to a portion of the [Patient Protection and] Affordable Care Act dealing with contraception.

Formally, the words are true. The court hasn't voted on the issue, and technically may not ever end up hearing it. So [the] thing for a lawyer to *say* is, "Thank you, Your Honor."

The correct thing to *think*, however, echoes George Orwell: "There are . . . about eighty ways in the English and American languages of expressing incredulity—for example, *garn, come off it, you bet, sez you, oh yeah, not half, I don't think, less of it* or *and the pudding!* But I think *and then you wake up* is the exactly suitable answer."

A Request for Exemption

As Cornell professor Michael Dorf explains, the court's grant of a stay to Little Sisters "suggests that, at least at this stage of the litigation, the plaintiffs have made out a colorable claim." The nature of that claim offers a glimpse of some toxic ideas floating around in American law.

What do the nuns object to? As Lyle Denniston of *SCO-TUSblog* explains, they object to the simple act of asking for a religious exemption to providing their lay employees with insurance coverage for contraceptive services. "The Little Sisters told the Supreme Court that even filing that form would make them a part of the scheme, and thus draw them into support for abortions or abortion-related services," Denniston writes.

The Little Sisters object to filling out the form even though they are a "church plan." This means, as the government noted in its brief, *their employees won't get contraceptive care no matter what form they fill out.* The third party running their health plan will be "under no legal obligation to provide the coverage after applicants certify that they object to providing it."

In other words, the Little Sisters want to be exempt from even *telling* the government that they are exempt from a plan that, in any case, would not require them to do anything they object to doing. Couple that with the pending claim by Hobby Lobby stores that a for-profit corporation has a "free exercise" right to block its employees from being compensated for contraceptive methods their employers object to. [The Hobby Lobby case,] which will be argued on March 25, was brought by corporations owning two retail chains. The stock is held by a conservative Christian family, the Greens, who believe that destroying a fertilized egg is the equivalent of killing a living person. The corporations demand exemption from the [Patient Protection and] Affordable Care Act's requirement that employee health insurance policies cover a full range of contraceptive options. The corporations are for-profit businesses that employee 13,000 people. They are being regulated as part of a general regulation of commerce. But their owners don't want to take part. Who is mere government to ask them to do so?

An Attempt to Opt Out

Taken together, these two cases aren't claims for religious exemption. They are more like an ordinance of secession—a statement that religious bodies, and people, and even commercial businesses, no longer belong to society if they decide they'd rather not. The idea depends on an assumption that government itself is sinful, and presumptively illegitimate. If courts follow this notion, they risk making it impossible to have an effective government at all. And ineffective or weak government, as Peter Shane explained here a few weeks ago, was not part of the founders' vision for America.

Nor is there any warrant in our history for blanket religious exemptions from social norms. Consider conscientious objection. When the people's representatives decide the nation is in danger, citizens may be asked give up their liberty and, if necessary, their lives to defend it. But in the United States, at least since World War I, religious people who object to war have been permitted to refuse to bear arms in their country's defense.

What they get, though, is not immunity. Instead, they have been required to certify their religious objection and, if necessary, prove that it is sincere. Then they have been required to perform alternate service—working in a hospital, for example, or in a national park—to aid the nation's survival in ways that do not involve personally killing. It is a compromise between conscience and the collective.

By analogy to the Little Sisters claim, however, truly devout conscientious objectors wouldn't be required to perform *any* service—since, of course, any service would contribute to the country that's at war. In fact, they would refuse to request an exemption; even filling out the form would make them complicit.

The assumption seems to be that religion releases you from any obligation of any kind to the state. And that's apparently even true if you are a giant for-profit corporation.

The Governmental Interest

I do not question that the nuns, and the Green family, are sincere. But why are they the only ones whose interest matter? These cases involve the government and the employees covered by the act. Their interests should count, too.

In the case of the Little Sisters, government has a clear interest in keeping track of which organizations claim exemptions and making sure those claims are genuine. What judge, until recently, would have thought that interest illegitimate?

In [the case of] Hobby Lobby in particular, the government has a powerful interest in making sure that its comprehensive insurance scheme provides uniform opportunities to all employees in commerce. That interest can sometimes overcome even the most sincere religious objection. In 1964, many people had sincere religious beliefs that African Americans and whites should not mix in restaurants, stores, and hotels—that this violated the words of Acts 17:26 that God had fixed boundaries for the nations of man and expected them to remain within them. (There are sincere believers of this idea even today within the so-called "British Israel" and "Christian Identity" sects.)

The Civil Rights Act did not demand that these people change their beliefs. It did not demand that they desegregate their churches, or open their homes. But it did embody a judgment by society that, in order to engage in business, they had to open their businesses to all.

The same kind of governmental interest is present in the contraceptive-mandate cases: If you want to engage in interstate commerce, cover your employees. The peoples' representatives have determined that both public health and the economy will function better if you do.

The Employees' Interests

And that brings in the employees' interests: first, in making their own health choices from a full range of options; second, in earning full benefits for their work, whether they are men or women; and finally—this one seems to be mentioned by almost no one—in their own religious liberty. For most of us, choices about contraception arise from our own consciences. In a free country, the boss doesn't collect the employees' beliefs at the workplace door.

The Tenth Circuit opinion upholding Hobby Lobby's supposed right to an exemption is a remarkable document. It does not say that the Greens' beliefs outweigh those of government and employees. It simply pretends that only the Greens have any interests at all. As Chief Judge Mary Briscoe points out in her dissent, the Tenth Circuit's opinion "does not mention the public interest that the government had relied on at the preliminary-injunction hearing: the health reasons for promoting employee access to emergency contraceptives." (Briscoe is the only woman on the court. The plurality of male judges did not balance women's health away—they just forgot it was an issue.)

How can it be that in a case concerning health care, health interests somehow don't matter? Whether among married or unmarried women, planned pregnancies produce better outcomes, both for mother and child and for the families involved. In other words, mothers raising children are healthier if they can space their pregnancies—and are less likely to have premature or low-birth-weight babies. Some women have chronic medical conditions and should never become pregnant; others need to manage their own health in order to prepare for pregnancy. And some contraceptive methods have important health benefits that don't relate to contraception at all.

To effectively make their health choices, women need not only "some" contraception, or only those methods that lay employers approve; they need access to the full spectrum of medically safe methods. The public's interest in their freedom to make those choices is huge. "There's a reason why the Centers for Disease Control and Prevention listed family planning as one of the 10 great public health achievements of the 20th century," Adam Sonfield, a senior public policy associate at the Guttmacher Institute, said in an interview.

And beyond the health question, for heaven's sake, think for a moment about "liberty": A country where employees have both jobs and religious freedom will be freer than one where they must choose between the two.

Periodical and Internet Sources Bibliography

The following articles have been selected to supplement the diverse views presented in this chapter.

John H. Cochrane	"The Real Trouble with the Birth-Control Mandate," *Wall Street Journal*, February 9, 2012.
Dahlia Lithwick	"Conscience Creep: What's So Wrong with Conscience Clauses?," *Slate*, October 3, 2013.
Katie McDonough	"5 Reasons the Contraception Mandate Matters for Everyone," *Salon*, January 6, 2014.
William Murchison	"The Theology of ObamaCare," *Human Life Review*, Winter 2012.
Sarah Posner	"More than a Hobby," *American Prospect*, July 18, 2013.
Sheldon Richman	"Dump the Contraception Mandate (and the Rest of Obamacare)," Reason.com, January 5, 2014.
David B. Rivkin Jr. and Edward Whelan	"Birth-Control Mandate: Unconstitutional and Illegal," *Wall Street Journal*, February 15, 2012.
Ilya Shapiro	"Symposium: Mandates Make Martyrs Out of Corporate Owners," *SCOTUSblog*, February 24, 2014.
Lois Uttley	"Employees Need Birth Control Coverage Mandate," *Nation*, February 17, 2012.
Matthew Vadum	"If the Left Knew Christians Were Coming They'd've Baked a Cake," *American Thinker*, March 1, 2014.
Jessica Valenti	"Birth Control Coverage: It's the Misogyny, Stupid," *Nation*, November 26, 2013.

CHAPTER 4

How Should Ethics
Guide Economic Policies?

Chapter Preface

Since the recession of the late 2000s, more and more public debate has focused on the level of economic inequality that exists in the United States. There is wide disagreement about whether inequality is a problem, and the issue was made no less polarizing when President Barack Obama remarked in December 2013 that "a dangerous and growing inequality and lack of upward mobility" exist in the United States and referred to the problem as "the defining challenge of our time."

According to data collected by the US Census Bureau, in 2012 the median household income was approximately $51,000, meaning that half of the households in the United States made less than this and half made more. However, the disparity between the top earners and lower earners was striking: The top 5 percent of households accounted for 22.3 percent of all income in 2012. The top 20 percent of households had 51 percent of all income, whereas the lowest 20 percent of households had only 3.2 percent of aggregate income.

Income is not the only marker of inequality. Household net worth, which measures the wealth of households by adding up all assets—such as house value, stocks, and savings accounts—and subtracting all debt—such as mortgage owed, student loans, and credit card debt—shows the inequality that exists not only in income, but in the wealth that households are able to accumulate. G. William Domhoff, a professor of sociology at the University of California, Santa Cruz, reports that the top 1 percent of households in 2010 had an average net worth of $16,439,400, and the top 20 percent of households had an average net worth of $2,061,600. He claims that the bottom 40 percent actually had an average household net worth of -$10,600, meaning that on average their debts outweighed any assets held. He says that in 2010 the top 20 percent of households in the United States owned 89 percent of all privately held wealth (with the top 1 percent accounting for 35 percent of all wealth), leaving 11 percent of total wealth for the bottom 80 percent of US households.

A national survey by the Pew Research Center and *USA Today*, conducted in January 2014, found that the majority of Americans (65 percent) believe that the gap between the rich and everyone else has increased in the past ten years. Even more than that—69 percent of Americans—believe that the government should be doing something to reduce this gap.

Opposing viewpoints exist about whether or not economic inequality is a problem in the United States. As the authors in this chapter show, there are strong views across the spectrum about the ethics of various economic policies, such as those that lead to inequality.

"The case for economic growth is largely indistinguishable from the case for economic progress; both are ultimately deeply normative."

It Should Be Recognized That Economic Policies Have Roots in Moral Philosophy

Robert H. Nelson

In the following viewpoint, Robert H. Nelson argues that although there is an illusion of moral neutrality in modern economics, in fact economics is full of value judgments. Nelson cites several historical economic thinkers to illustrate the moral philosophy underpinning economic theory. He claims that modern economics clings to the idea that economic growth is the absolute value and that this idea ought to be examined and challenged. Nelson is a professor of environmental policy at the University of Maryland and the author of The New Holy Wars: Economic Religion vs. Environmental Religion in Contemporary America.

As you read, consider the following questions:

1. The author cites what term as a relatively new connotation for the phenomenon that was once called progress?

Robert H. Nelson, "The Secular Religions of Progress," *New Atlantis*, no. 39, Summer 2013, pp. 38–43, 47–50. Copyright © 2013 by The New Atlantis. All rights reserved. Reproduced by permission.

2. According to Nelson, what did philosopher Jeremy Bentham say is the supreme goal of the moral philosopher?

3. Nelson contends that economic estimates and projections frequently leave out short-term costs, citing what examples?

Economics has never been, nor could it ever be, free of value judgments. The economy is not isolated from the rest of society, cordoned off from the lively world of competing beliefs. Rather, questions of the organization of the economy, and of the economic policies to be pursued, are interwoven with other social concerns and public policy in general. Economists often lose sight of the altogether interconnected nature of the economic and the non-economic. The illusion of neutrality is reinforced by the radical simplification that often characterizes economic methods; in striving to make economic problems tractable for mathematical representation, inherent ethical considerations are obscured.

The Definition of Progress

Some of the greatest economists of earlier eras, like Adam Smith and John Stuart Mill, regarded themselves as moral philosophers, as analysts of the moral foundations of society. Few contemporary economists see themselves in such a light. If they do take moral considerations into account, it is typically as parameters for subsequent economic analysis.

As a result, the powerful normative elements of economics tend to be driven underground. Economists today become *implicit* moral philosophers, a point the University of Illinois economist Deirdre McCloskey often emphasizes. Most economists, for example, regard economic growth as a main goal of the economic system, and seek to assess the desirability of public policies by the extent to which they are efficient or inefficient toward that end. Whether growth should itself be a paramount objective, and whether efficiency should therefore play such a critical role in distinguishing between good and bad policy, typically receives little sustained attention among mainstream economists, with few exceptions (such as Herman Daly in his 1996 book *Beyond Growth*).

Economic growth is actually a relatively recent term for a phenomenon that was once called "progress." The creation of the American economics profession began with the founding of the American Economic Association in 1885 and was a product of the Progressive Era. Progressives believed that scientific experts, including professional economists, should engineer society toward a better future. But moral and economic crises in the 1930s and 1940s called into question the Progressives' basic methods and aspirations, giving reason to leave behind the morally freighted language of "progress." By the second half of the twentieth century, historians increasingly characterized the thought of the Progressive Era in such terms as "the gospel of efficiency." A new greater emphasis on technical economic efficiency, along with the closely related concept of growth, recast progress in more scientific and mathematical, and less emotionally and ideologically weighted, language. But the terminological substitution of "growth" for "progress" makes little difference. The case for economic growth is largely indistinguishable from the case for economic progress; both are ultimately deeply normative.

But why is progress, or growth, desirable? Progress means improvement, and so its desirability is in a sense tautological, but economic growth is thought of specifically as the increase in material outputs—the maximization of the production and consumption of goods and services. To understand why this goal is considered desirable today, we must look back over the major economic theories of modernity. Although the survey that follows will sometimes paint in very broad strokes, it will show just how strongly these economic theories draw on moral philosophy and especially on religious thought. Some theories could even be said to constitute secular religions in their own right, implying "theologies" of evil and of the human condition, of redemption, and ultimately of a final paradise, which we achieve through economic growth.

The Economist as a Moral Philosopher

Adam Smith was a pivotal figure in the transition from traditional Christianity to secular religion. In Smith's *Theory of Moral Sentiments* (1759), there is, as University of Chicago economist Jacob Viner keenly observed, "an unqualified doctrine of a harmonious order of nature, under divine guidance, which promotes the welfare of man through the operation of his individual propensities." In Smith's later work *The Wealth of Nations* (1776), he was less forthcoming about the divine ordering of nature, but the underlying moral philosophy was fundamentally similar.

The term "natural" recurs throughout *The Wealth of Nations* as a normative basis for judgments on economic processes and outcomes. "Natural" means the natural order of the world, as established by God, which we fallen human beings can only imperfectly understand but to which we should strive to conform as best we can. Smith could express his conception of economic processes as a divine natural harmony largely in secular terms, drawing on the Newtonian [referring to Sir Isaac Newton] understanding of the universe as a complex mechanism put in motion by God. Much as gravity was the force that maintained order for Newton in the physical universe, self-interest holds up both moral and economic order for Smith.

The Wealth of Nations was thus a new development in secular religion, ultimately grounded in the natural law theology that had long been prominent especially in the Catholic tradition. In Smith, it was combined with a Calvinist [referring to the Christian teachings of John Calvin that stress God's power and the moral weakness of human beings] sense of the human condition as deeply corrupted. But even though most human beings were frail and foolish, pursuing their own interests without regard to the needs of the wider community, God had benevolently arranged for society to thrive and advance toward its greater welfare.

Smith was writing for a world in which Christian values suffused every area of society. As secularism increased in the centuries that followed, the advancement of these values would come to depend on separating them from traditional religion and its historic institutions, while instead embedding them— even if thereby distorting them—in various forms of secular religion. By mostly omitting explicit references to a Christian God, *The Wealth of Nations*, with its newly secularized account of a divine balance of natural forces in society, was in an ideal position to become a major influence on future economists.

Among twentieth-century economists, the University of Chicago's Frank Knight was the closest to Smith as a moral philosopher. Knight was a key figure in founding the "Chicago school of economics," which typically advocated the organization of society along free-market lines. After Knight, however, few Chicago economists wrote about the market in explicitly moral and religious terms, although the moral and religious elements maintained a powerful implicit presence.

The Greatest Good

Jeremy Bentham, a younger contemporary of Smith, developed a very different moral philosophy. Whereas Smith helped put the Western natural law tradition on a secular footing, Bentham famously described the idea of natural rights as "nonsense upon stilts." The notion that there were laws of nature governing human affairs seemed ludicrous to him; rather, Bentham argued, human life is ordered by social conventions that are shaped by the forces of pleasure and pain.

For Bentham, the supreme goal of the moral philosopher is to discover which conventions maximize the happiness (understood in hedonistic terms) of the greatest number of people and thereby to judge the utility—that is to say, in his terms the ethical status—of any action. Inspired by the rise of the natural sciences, Bentham saw his utilitarian theories as part of a new scientific understanding of the sources of happiness in society. By putting the social sciences to work, rapid progress in society, including in the economic realm, would soon yield much greater overall personal happiness and collective well-being.

By defining ultimate objectives in strictly human terms, Bentham took a large step toward atheistic moral philosophy. While Smith invoked the guiding hand of a deity, for Bentham the future of mankind lay directly in human hands. As secularism continued to rise in the eighteenth century, the true source of human misbehavior—of "evil" in the classical Christian formulation—was seen by Enlightenment thinkers increasingly in environmental terms (here using the word "environment" not in its ecological sense but in its more general sense). Human beings were not innately bad owing to a moral fall in the distant past; instead, harmful environments made people bad. This notion introduced a hope that would become a central element of secular religion: improving the quality of the environment would naturally lead to an improvement in the quality of human lives. The world would be a far happier place and individual people much less likely to cheat, steal, or commit other immoral acts. With the economy as the newly decisive environmental factor, economics seemingly could save the world.

Bentham's utilitarian moral philosophy provided the grounds for a host of social reforms in nineteenth-century England, many of which Bentham successfully pushed for himself. If Smith was an advocate of individual market freedom, Bentham's utilitarianism was a precursor to modern democratic socialism, applied as the foundation for a science of affirmative governance. Even today, the standard forms of economic analysis are framed in utilitarian terms ultimately derived from Bentham and his greatest disciple, John Stuart Mill. Economic growth is central to such conceptions, not as the objective in itself, but as a necessary means to maximum total consumption—and thus to a society's greatest welfare.

Twentieth-century economics adopted a revised version of Bentham's utilitarianism, no longer arguing that the level of happiness itself is scientifically explainable or measurable, but focusing instead on the fact that human beings identify various material outcomes as preferable to others. Economists still followed after Bentham, however, in thinking that the study of individual behavior can and should be a matter for science, that the real basis for individual happiness lies in consumption of goods and services, and that the comprehensive application of economic knowledge (with that of other social sciences) would lead to maximum happiness, the ultimate goal of society.

Positivism and the Religion of Humanity

In the first half of the nineteenth century, another school of economic and political thought arose that pushed toward the creation of what was, quite literally, a secular religion. The French positivists, led by Henri de Saint-Simon and Auguste Comte, again believed that social science would achieve a comprehensive scientific understanding of human affairs. As social science was perfected, a much more effective management of society, and thereby of its productive machinery, would increasingly become feasible.

This optimistic hope for man's ability to engineer the economy echoes an element of Smith's theory: the systematic application of science would solve the problems of society. And like Bentham, the French positivists believed that government would be able to put the new scientific understanding of society to work for the perfection of the human condition.

Moreover, the positivists shared with Bentham the belief that traditional deities and religions are simply myths or fictions. In their place, the positivists envisioned a new secular "religion of humanity," one based on social and physical science. Saint-Simon dreamed of temples dedicated to Newton, while Comte came to think of himself as the pope of the new religion of humanity. The high priests of French positivism were the economists and engineers.

The American Progressive movement at the end of the nineteenth century and the start of the twentieth drew much of its inspiration from the moral philosophy of French positivism. The Progressives shared the positivists' commitment to the management and governance of society by its scientific experts, now to be produced in large numbers by the modern American university with its newly professionalized structures of learning. The Progressives also held a negative view of ordinary politics as a frequently backward and harmful influence that should as much as possible be excluded from the governing processes of the economy; economic growth, rather than politics, would be the font of both material gain and moral progress. The Progressives' materialistic dogmas and their doctrines of economic determinism saw all of history as fundamentally driven by economic events.

The twentieth-century British economist John Maynard Keynes shared this moral philosophy in significant part, but he differed in one key respect. Rather than implementing scientific management directly through governmental actions—the path of socialism—Keynes believed that the progressive goals of society should instead be achieved by the management of the workings of the marketplace—the market "mechanism," to use the revealing term popularized by Paul Samuelson. By discovering the "laws" of the market, economic theorists could lay the same kind of foundation for economic and social engineering that the laws of physics establish for building bridges. This positivistic vision of science as a means to achieve progress is still a key part of the self-image of mainstream economists, a reflection of American progressive values derived originally from the secular religion of French positivism.

With the emphasis on efficient maximization of economic production, the positivist moral philosophy makes economic growth a central objective. But its ultimate concern is the scientific management of society. If the social order is designed, operated, and maintained according to the impersonal dictates of objective scientific knowledge, it will wipe away the many social conflicts that flow from our long-standing ignorance of how society really works. Of course, this social reordering would first entail citizens' acceptance of the comprehensive direction of scientific experts—a transformation in our political system that would likely require a religious revolution of the sort that the positivists, with their secular religion of humanity, thought desirable and necessary....

The Costs of Economic Gains

The general lack of attention in mainstream economics to issues of moral philosophy limits economists' recognition of the central role that a powerful progressive value system plays in their own field, not only in making policy recommendations but in underpinning the core methods of economic analysis. With very few exceptions—such as Harvard's Benjamin M. Friedman, author of the 2005 book *The Moral Consequences of Economic Growth*—economists seldom compare the benefits of economic growth with the costs, usually assuming automatically that the former outweigh the latter.

But growth radically transforms society—and not always for the better. Economic gains often come hand in hand with personal, social, cultural, and environmental losses that economists too easily ignore; it is simpler to make judgments about what is economically beneficial based on quantifiable factors and impersonal market mechanisms. Consider trade with

China. It has no doubt helped to increase total available goods and services in the United States and has produced large material benefits in China too. But it has thrown many American workers out of their jobs and undermined the vitality of many U.S. communities. How can we say that the social gains of U.S. trade with China are greater than the social costs? Many economists find it easy to answer this question, assuming that economic progress, given its necessarily transcendent importance over any social costs incurred, must always be worth it.

This, however, is not a scientific conclusion but rather one based on a secular-religious faith in the absolute value of economic growth and efficiency. Few if any economists have sought to do a truly comprehensive cost-benefit analysis of trade with China—one in which the costs have included the psychic demoralization of workers who have lost their jobs and of owners whose businesses have failed, and the transitional costs (not just economic but again, psychic) associated with the disruption of workers having to move their families from one community to another. These hidden costs are not easy to measure, but that does not mean they are unimportant, and it is only a blinding devotion to growth that obscures them from economic analysis.

Moreover, economic estimates and projections of growth frequently leave out short-term costs, the stresses and strains that arise in the process of creative destruction, while focusing entirely on the long term. The range of short-run costs that economic analyses normally ignore includes not just the financial and psychic losses when a worker loses a job, but also the loss of community when the market renders a negative verdict on the mainstays of a local economy; the loss of homes, streets, farms, and other historic treasures; the transformation of plant and animal habitats into resources for exploitation; the weakening of communal bonds; the feelings of personal powerlessness when private organizations are the efficiency winners in the market, leaving many people to work as small parts in large and often impersonal bureaucratic enterprises; and the diminishment of personal freedom associated with the kind of government regulation and taxation put in place to sustain and promote economic activity. There is also the sense that some assets or activities are devalued by the very fact of entering them into the price system as goods and services—the commodification of human reproduction, for instance. (In a few cases, such as prostitution, government intervenes to limit the devaluing consequences of commodification, but these are the exceptions that prove the rule.)

Admittedly, it would be impossible to assign monetary values to many of these costs. But the more fundamental issue is that economic analyses systematically and deliberately leave them out of consideration, focusing instead on achieving the path of the maximum growth of the economy, the path to heaven on earth. If one were able to account for the costs in every dimension associated with gains in economic progress and efficiency, we might find that the gains are not always worth the costs.

The Argument for Economic Growth

In parts of the world that are less developed than the United States—in countries like Cambodia or Haiti, for example—it is not difficult to make a strong argument for both the material and moral benefits of economic growth. But what about in the United States today? Perhaps a century ago the countless beneficial social transformations that recent economic development had produced might have offered strong grounds for holding to the faith that growth is a paramount good. But in the twenty-first century, the case for unlimited growth in already economically developed countries may have become less obvious. Why, then, does it remain such a central goal in American politics? To some extent it may be a matter of inertia: We have all agreed about the need for growth for so long, even in the midst of our disagreements about capitalism versus socialism—which can be seen as disagreements about how best to achieve growth—that we cannot easily refocus our politics on some other fundamental good. Also, the growth agenda has played a unifying role in American culture. A nation as large as the United States needs a "civil religion" to hold it together, as the late Robert Bellah argued. Although its hold has been weakening, the American civil religion still assigns a central role to the importance of economic growth. Absent a good substitute, it might be dangerous to give up on so central a part of the American faith.

Of course, a moral argument can still easily be made for progress in such areas as human health. But an argument for advancing medicine and improving health care is not an argument for general economic progress, but rather for devoting more of our society's resources to the health sector. And more practically, growth seems the only way we have at present of dealing with the problem of unemployment. Theoretically, in times of insufficient total aggregate demand, there could be a cooperative agreement in society that each working person should reduce his or her workforce participation by a sufficient amount to allow every person to be employed. But this would entail, to put it mildly, immense political and practical difficulties. So growth may be all we currently have as a unifying solution that can deal with unemployment.

What are the alternatives to growth? What could replace the secular religions of progress? The leading challenge to our faith in growth, the environmental movement, is only a few decades old. Moreover, environmentalists' critique of progressive economic utopianism and other forms of economic religion is often more impressive than their positive vision for the future. It is not hard to imagine that the alternatives to growth espoused by the environmentalists, such as a static or even retracting economy, might carry along with it a civilizational ennui or enervation.

Looking beyond the economic progressivism that has played such a large role in American history, it may be that rather than the elimination of material scarcity, the central theme of our future civil religion should be the maintenance of human freedom. Such an approach could draw on ideas that Adam Smith articulated but that were de-emphasized in some of the subsequent economic moral philosophies. Whatever economic model we subscribe to, we would do well to acknowledge its religious qualities—the extent to which it affects our understanding of the human condition, of how good ought to overcome evil, and even of our eschatological hopes. Professional economists in particular should learn to recognize and make explicit that their commitments to economic systems have deep roots in moral philosophy.

| "We have created a society in which materialism overwhelms moral commitment."

Morality Requires Reform of the Current Economic System

Joseph E. Stiglitz

In the following viewpoint, Joseph E. Stiglitz argues that the global economic crisis exposed deep problems with market fundamentalism. Stiglitz contends that the deceptive practices employed by the financial sector exposed how moral depravity governs the system, where any action that is technically legal is seen as beyond rebuke, and he argues for the need for the financial sector to accept blame. Stiglitz is a professor at Columbia University and the author of The Price of Inequality: How Today's Divided Society Endangers Our Future.

As you read, consider the following questions:

1. Stiglitz claims that over thirty years ago corporations used to accept that corporate leaders should be paid beyond the average worker by what factor?

Joseph E. Stiglitz, "Moral Bankruptcy: Why Are We Letting Wall Street Off So Easy?," *Mother Jones* online, January/February 2010. www.motherjones.com. Copyright © 2010 by Mother Jones. All rights reserved. Reproduced by permission.

2. The author contends that corporations often claim that decisions about right and wrong are not up to them but up to whom?

3. Stiglitz argues that failures in the financial system are emblematic of what broader failures?

It is said that a near-death experience forces one to reevaluate priorities and values. The global economy has just escaped a near-death experience. The crisis exposed the flaws in the prevailing economic model, but it also exposed flaws in our society. Much has been written about the foolishness of the risks that the financial sector undertook, the devastation that its institutions have brought to the economy, and the fiscal deficits that have resulted. Too little has been written about the underlying moral deficit that has been exposed—a deficit that is larger, and harder to correct.

The Impact of Market Fundamentalism

One of the lessons of this crisis is that there is a need for collective action, that there is a role for government. But there are others. We allowed markets to blindly shape our economy, but in doing so, they also shaped our society. We should take this opportunity to ask: Are we sure that the way that they have been molding us is what we want?

We have created a society in which materialism overwhelms moral commitment, in which the rapid growth that we have achieved is not sustainable environmentally or socially, in which we do not act together to address our common needs. Market fundamentalism has eroded any sense of community and has led to rampant exploitation of unwary and unprotected individuals. There has been an erosion of trust—and not just in our financial institutions. It is not too late to close these fissures.

How the market has altered the way we think is best illustrated by attitudes toward pay. There used to be a social contract about the reasonable division of the gains that arise from acting together within the economy. Within corporations, the pay of the leader might be 10 or 20 times that of the average worker. But something happened 30 years ago, as the era of Thatcher/Reagan [United Kingdom prime minister Margaret Thatcher and US president Ronald Reagan] was ushered in. There ceased to be any sense of fairness; it was simply how much the executive could appropriate for himself. It became perfectly respectable to call it incentive pay, even when there was little relationship between pay and performance. In the finance sector, when performance is high, pay is high; but when performance is low, pay is still high. The bankers knew—or should have known—that while high leverage might generate high returns in good years, it also exposed the banks to large downside risks. But they also knew that under their contracts, this would not affect their bonuses.

A Likelihood of Deception

What happens when reward is decoupled from risk? One cannot always distinguish between incompetence and deception, but it seems unlikely that a business claiming to have a net worth of more than $100 billion could suddenly find itself in negative territory. More likely than not, it was engaged in deceptive accounting practices. Similarly, it is hard to believe that the mortgage originators and the investment bankers didn't know that the products they were creating, purchasing, and repackaging were toxic.

[Ponzi scheme operator] Bernie Madoff crossed the line between exaggeration and fraudulent behavior. But what about Angelo Mozilo, the former head of Countrywide Financial, the nation's largest originator of subprime mortgages? He has been charged by the SEC [US Securities and Exchange Commission] with securities fraud and insider trading: He privately described the mortgages he was originating as toxic, even saying that Countrywide was "flying blind," all while touting the strengths of his mortgage company, its prime quality mortgages using high underwriting standards. He eventually sold his Countrywide stock for nearly $140 million in profits. If he had kept the dirty secrets to himself, he might have been spared the charges; self-deception is no crime, nor is persuading others to share in that self-deception. The lesson for future financiers is simple: Don't share your innermost doubts.

The investment bankers would like us to believe that they were deceived by the people who sold them the mortgages. But if there was deception, they were part of it: They encouraged the mortgage originators to go into the risky subprime market, because it generated the high returns they sought. It is possible that a few bankers didn't know what they were doing, but they are guilty then of a different crime, that of misrepresentation, claiming that they knew about risk when clearly they did not.

Exaggerating the virtues of one's wares or claiming greater competency than the evidence warrants is something that one might have expected from many businesses. Far harder to forgive is the moral depravity—the financial sector's exploitation of poor and middle-class Americans. Our financial system discovered that there was money at the bottom of the pyramid and did everything possible to move it toward the top. We are still debating why the regulators didn't stop this. But shouldn't the question also have been: Didn't those engaging in these practices have any moral compunction?

The Issue of Legality

Sometimes, the financial companies (and other corporations) say that it is not up to them to make the decisions about what is right and wrong. It is up to government. So long as the government hasn't banned the activity, a bank has every obligation to its shareholders to provide financial support for any activity from which it can obtain a good return. The predeces-

Milt Priggee, "Inequality for All," Cagle Cartoons.

sors to JPMorgan Chase helped finance slave purchases. Citibank had no qualms about staying in apartheid South Africa.

But consider, too, that the business community spends large amounts of money trying to create legislation that allows it to engage in nefarious practices. The financial sector worked hard to stop predatory lending laws, to gut state consumer protection laws, and to ensure that the federal government's ever laxer standards overrode state regulators. Their ideal scenario, it seems, is to have the kind of regulation that doesn't prevent them from doing anything, but allows them to say, in case of any problems, that they assumed everything was okay—because it was done within the law.

Securitization epitomized the process of how markets can weaken personal relationships and community. With securitization, trust has no role; the lender and the borrower have no personal relationship. Everything is anonymous, and with those whose lives are being destroyed represented as merely data, the only issues in restructuring are what is legal—what is the mortgage servicer allowed to do—and what will maximize the expected return to the owners of the securities. Enmeshed in legal tangles, both lenders and borrowers suffer. Only the lawyers win.

This crisis has exposed fissures between Wall Street and Main Street, between America's rich and the rest of our society. Over the last two decades, incomes of most Americans have stagnated. We papered over the consequences by telling those at the bottom—and those in the middle—to continue to consume as if there had been an increase; they were encouraged to live beyond their means, by borrowing; and the bubble made it possible.

The Need for Change

The country as a whole has been living beyond its means. There will have to be some adjustment. And someone will have to pick up the tab for the bank bailouts. With real median household income already down some 4 percent between 2000 and 2008, the brunt of the adjustment must come from those at the top who have garnered for themselves so much over the past three decades, and from the financial sector, which has imposed such high costs on the rest of society.

But the politics of this will not be easy. The financial sector is reluctant to own up to its failings. Part of moral behavior and individual responsibility is to accept blame when it is due. Yet bankers have repeatedly worked hard to shift blame to others, including to those they victimized. In today's financial markets, almost everyone claims innocence. They were all just doing their jobs. There was individualism, but no individual responsibility.

Some have argued that we had a problem in our financial plumbing. Our pipes got clogged, and we needed federal intervention to get the markets moving again. So we called in the same plumbers who installed the plumbing—having created the mess, presumably only they knew how to straighten it out. Never mind if they overcharged us for the installation, then overcharged us for the repair. We should quietly pay the bills, and pray that they did a better job this time than last.

But it is more than a matter of unclogging a drain. The failures in our financial system are emblematic of broader failures in our economic system and our society. That there will be changes as a result of the crisis is certain. The question is, will they be in the right direction? Over the past decade, we have altered not only our institutions—encouraging ever more bigness in finance—but the very rules of capitalism. We have announced that for favored institutions there is to be little or no market discipline. We have created an ersatz capitalism, socializing losses as we privatize gains, a system with unclear rules, but with a predictable outcome: future crises, undue risk-taking at the public expense, and greater inefficiency.

It has become a cliché to observe that the Chinese characters for crisis reflect "danger" and "opportunity." We have seen the danger. Will we seize the opportunity?

> "Only the moral case for freedom and opportunity . . . will have a chance to save the American experiment that we say we want."

The Free Market Is the Only Moral Economic System

Arthur C. Brooks

In the following viewpoint, Arthur C. Brooks argues that there is a moral case for free enterprise. Brooks contends that America was founded on principles that support little government interference with the market. He argues that Americans have the right to earned success, fairness, and a system that lifts the poor. Brooks contends that free enterprise is the only system that can guarantee this freedom and opportunity. Brooks is the president of the American Enterprise Institute and the author of The Road to Freedom: How to Win the Fight for Free Enterprise.

As you read, consider the following questions:

1. Brooks claims that America's founders were not materialists, but rather were what?

2. According to Brooks, what is earned success?

3. What does Brooks say is responsible for the reduction between 1970 and 2010 in the number of people worldwide who live on less than a dollar a day?

Earlier this month [October 2012] in the first presidential debate, Mitt Romney made an unusual argument by modern political standards: that long-term deficit spending is not just an economic issue, but a moral one. "I think it's . . . not moral for my generation to keep spending massively more than we take in, knowing those burdens are going to be passed on to the next generation."

A Moral Defense of Free Enterprise

This is a notable occurrence, not just because Romney is frequently chided for being cool and detached, but because it represents a return to something our founders knew but succeeding generations have forgotten: Limited government and individual liberty aren't merely policy alternatives. They're moral imperatives.

America's founders were moralists, not materialists. The Declaration of Independence defends not our right to material prosperity, but, rather, the covenant between government and citizens of "life, liberty, and the pursuit of happiness." In both public declarations as well as personal correspondence, the founders discussed, debated, and explained their thinking using moral language.

In today's commercial republic, the freedom our founders fought for is expressed in the form of free enterprise: the system of laws and institutions that rewards entrepreneurship and hard work, largely on the basis of markets and competition. Free enterprise is what Thomas Jefferson meant by the "free exercise of industry . . . and the fruits acquired by it." Free enterprise is compatible with government in the case of market failures (such as crime) and a safety net for the indigent, but it is inconsistent with today's growing statism and corporate cronyism.

Today, we rarely hear a moral defense for free enterprise from our politicians, which is why Romney's statement was so striking. And the general lack of moral defense explains why—despite the fact that surveys find a large majority of Americans think the government is too big and trying to do too much—we acquiesce to larger and larger government from both parties. Indeed, it is why government at all levels has grown from 15 percent of U.S. GDP [gross domestic product] in 1940 to more than 35 percent today, and—according to the Congressional Budget Office—will hit 50 percent in 2038.

Day after day, politicians offer one government benefit after another to our citizens. This has made a majority of Americans into net beneficiaries of the welfare state, as my colleague Nicholas Eberstadt chronicles in his new book, *A Nation of Takers*. While most Americans dislike the crisis and culture this has brought us, few are eager to give up their benefits. It is not compelling enough to point out that these goodies will lead to fiscal problems sometime in the future. It isn't even enough to scare citizens with threats of a Greek-style debt crisis, which will surely come if we continue to build a Greek-style social democracy with Greek-sized government.

The Moral Case for Freedom and Opportunity

Only the moral case for freedom and opportunity—the case that stimulated the struggle of our founders—will have a chance to save the American experiment that we say we want. That case requires that we make three arguments.

First, we have to argue for the right of every American to earn his or her success. Earned success does not mean making money. It means creating value with our lives, and in the lives of other people. For some, this means starting a for-profit business; for others, it means creating a beautiful work of art, raising great kids, or helping others. Regardless, there is a tre-

Free Enterprise

What is free enterprise? It is the system of values and laws that respects private property and limits government, encourages competition and industry, celebrates achievement based on merit, and creates individual opportunity. Under free enterprise, people can pursue their own ends, and they reap the rewards and consequences, positive and negative, of their own actions. Free enterprise requires trust in markets to produce the most desirable outcomes for society. It is the opposite of *statism*, which is the belief that the government is generally the best, fairest, and most trustworthy entity to distribute resources and coordinate our economic lives.

Arthur C. Brooks, The Road to Freedom:
How to Win the Fight for Free Enterprise.
New York: Basic Books, 2012.

mendous amount of evidence that people who say they have earned their success are our happiest citizens.

For earned success, we need a system that matches our skills and passions, rewards hard work, and lets us keep these rewards. If not, we will suffer what the eminent University of Pennsylvania psychologist Martin Seligman calls "learned helplessness." This is a condition in which our earned rewards are stripped away, or we are given something we have not earned. When we learn helplessness, we become passive and unhappy.

Second, we have to argue for basic fairness. For most Americans, a fair society is one in which hard work, creativity, and honest competition result in financial reward. It does not mean that we redistribute resources through government power just to get more equality. It also does not mean rewarding the government's cronies in favored industries—from green energy, to banks, to labor unions. It means rewarding merit and creating opportunity. It does not mean insider dealing, social engineering, equalizing economic outcomes, and pork-barrel spending.

Third, we have to argue for the rights of the poor, and fight for the system that lifts them up by the billions. Between 1970 and 2010, the percentage of the world's population living on less than a dollar a day has been reduced by about 80 percent. What explains this miracle? The United Nations or International Monetary Fund? U.S. foreign aid? Of course not. It was globalization, free trade, entrepreneurship, property rights, and the rule of law spreading around the world.

The Answer Is Free Enterprise

So what is the system that satisfies our demand to let people earn their success, that is fair, and that lifts up the poor by the billions? There is only one: free enterprise.

Two hundred years ago, Jefferson wrote: "The last hope of human liberty in this world rests on us." That is as true today as it was then. Free enterprise is America's blessing, and our gift to the world. Yet it is in peril, and only a moral defense will save America from squandering it as we follow the ruinous path of our European allies. We need more politicians, intellectuals, activists, and everyday Americans to stand up for free enterprise—not just because it makes us better off, but because it makes us better.

| "Let's raise the minimum wage to make it easier to reform the process and ultimately reduce the subsidies for those who do as we ask and fulfill their part of the social contract."

There Is a Moral and Economic Case for Raising the Minimum Wage

Norm Ornstein

In the following viewpoint, Norm Ornstein argues that there is a strong argument for raising the current federal minimum wage. Ornstein claims that for many people working at full-time jobs for minimum wage, there is no way for them to make ends meet except by taking government subsidies. Ornstein contends that the social contract demands that employment pay enough for people to live decent lives, and he argues that raising the minimum wage can help eliminate the need for government welfare. Ornstein is a political scientist and resident scholar at the American Enterprise Institute.

As you read, consider the following questions:

1. According to the author, there are efforts under way in California to raise the minimum wage to what by 2016?

2. What is the annual income of a person working full time at the federal minimum wage, according to the author?

3. In what manner does Ornstein say that the web of subsides and the current minimum wage can create disincentives to work?

One of the most interesting recent political and policy developments is the involvement of Ron Unz in a major effort on behalf of a referendum to raise California's minimum wage to $12 an hour by 2016.

The Minimum Wage

Unz, a libertarian Silicon Valley entrepreneur, previously shot to fame by successfully pushing a referendum to replace bilingual education in California with English-immersion programs (which led to a sharp rise in SAT scores). He also ran for the GOP nomination for governor of California in 1994, losing to then incumbent Pete Wilson.

Why would Unz, who has written regularly for the *American Conservative* (he served as publisher until recently), favor an increase in the minimum wage, when one would be hard-pressed to find a single Republican in Congress who would do so? He says, "We have all these low-wage workers who are getting $7.50, $8, or $9 an hour, and because they earn such small wages, the government subsidizes them with billions or tens of billions of dollars of social-welfare spending that comes from the taxpayer. It's a classic example of businesses privatizing the benefits of their workers while socializing the costs." McDonald's recently took his point one giant step further by urging its low-wage employees to get food stamps.

The past few weeks [in fall 2013] have brought an intense focus and discussion on the minimum wage, at the national as well as local and state levels. Rep. George Miller, D-Calif., and Sen. Tom Harkin, D-Iowa, both longtime champions of increasing the minimum wage, have a bill to raise it nationally to $10.10—still leaving the earning power lower than it was in 1968 when the minimum wage was $1.60. In New Jersey, a proposition to raise the state minimum wage to $8.25 and index it to inflation passed handily over the opposition of Gov. Chris Christie. Indeed, 19 states have higher minimum wages than the national one of $7.25 an hour (nine states have either a lower rate than the national figure or no minimum at all). In Washington State, a local referendum in the community of SeaTac, home of the Seattle airport, to raise the minimum wage to $15 passed narrowly over the intense opposition of the business community. We now have a body of research by top-flight economists showing that an increase in the minimum wage does not reduce employment or significantly hinder the economy.

The recent focus is in part because of some clear realities in the contemporary, sluggish American economy. One is that where jobs exist, they tend to be at the lower end of the scale. A second is that no one with a family working full time at the minimum wage can possibly survive without major assistance. Keep in mind that if one works 40 hours a week, 52 weeks a year at $7.25 an hour, that means an annual income of $15,080—assuming no time off and no sick days. Can any of us imagine trying to house, clothe, and feed a family—while paying for transportation to work, health insurance, and other necessities of life, much less going to an occasional movie—on $15,080 a year, or $13,926 after FICA [Federal Insurance Contributions Act] deductions? Imagine paying market rates for rent in the D.C. area, where a tiny apartment might take up two-thirds of the income, and require an hour or longer commute to get into the city, with subway costs taking up an additional 10 percent or more. Not much left for food or other necessities, even with a zero income tax rate. Imagine if you need child care!

Public Supports Raising Minimum Wage

Increasing Minimum Wage from $7.25 to $10.10 an hour	Total* %
Favor	73
Oppose	25
Don't know	3

* Figures may not add to 100% because of rounding.
Source: Pew Research Center/USA Today. Survey conducted Jan. 15–19, 2014.

TAKEN FROM: "Most See Inequality Growing, but Partisans Differ over Solutions," Pew Research Center, January 23, 2014.

The Web of Subsidies

Here is the infamous Mitt Romney quote from the 2012 campaign: "There are 47 percent of the people who will vote for the president no matter what. All right, there are 47 percent who are with him, who are dependent upon government, who believe that they are victims, who believe the government has a responsibility to care for them, who believe that they are entitled to health care, to food, to housing, to you name it—that that's an entitlement. And the government should give it to them. And they will vote for this president no matter what. . . . These are people who pay no income tax. . . . [M]y job is not to worry about those people. I'll never convince them they should take personal responsibility and care for their lives." That 47 percent includes those working at or near the minimum wage.

Whether or not most of those who work 40 hours a week at the minimum wage or near it and are supporting families believe that they are entitled to food and housing, the fact is that they are doing what we have long believed was fulfilling our basic social contract—work hard, be productive, and you and your family can live a decent life with a place to live, food on the table, clothes on your backs, and other necessities. In the past, Republicans thought that the market ought to set wages, and that a combination of government devices—including the earned-income tax credit [EITC], housing subsidies, food stamps, Medicaid, and other social-welfare programs—could fill in the gaps to make that social contract work, while also trying to remove disincentives from work via welfare reform. There is not only a continuing belief in some quarters that markets should set wages, but strenuous efforts to make deep cuts to food-stamp funding and slash other programs that help low-income workers—condemned as "takers."

It is a fact that our economic system continues to have big gaps. The web of subsidies can create real disincentives for those at the bottom of the scale who want to work but would actually lose more benefits than their minimum-wage income would bring in. The effective marginal tax rate for a couple both making low wages if the second person works can be more than 100 percent because of benefit formulas. A couple of weeks ago, when I wrote about the war on food stamps, I mentioned a D.C. woman who is struggling to feed herself and her daughter, but calculated that she would need a job paying $15 an hour to do better. That is an artifact of poorly constructed, patchwork policies. Liberal cant notwithstanding, there is a culture of dependency that can discourage work among many. But the fact is most people out of work want to work—it defines their self-worth.

How about a new approach? Let's try to alter the incentive structure to make work pay, while maintaining devices like EITC, rent subsidies, and the health insurance subsidies under the [Patient Protection and] Affordable Care Act so that those who are working can support their families and live decent lives. As Jared Bernstein has written, let's provide a tax credit when two people in a family want to work so that their work pays. Let's do more robust job training instead of cutting funding, and experiment with innovations like the German apprenticeship program and their work-sharing policy. And let's raise the minimum wage to make it easier to reform the process and ultimately reduce the subsidies for those who do as we ask and fulfill their part of the social contract.

> *"Far from being raised, all minimum
> wage laws should be condemned as im-
> moral and abolished."*

Minimum Wage Laws Are Immoral and Harmful

Ari Armstrong

*In the following viewpoint, Ari Armstrong argues that the de-
mand to raise the minimum wage is misguided and shows what
is wrong with having a minimum wage at all. He claims that a
minimum wage forces employers to pay employees more than
they may be worth, leading to fewer jobs for employees and
higher prices for consumers. Armstrong contends that minimum
wage laws are based on the fallacious moral claim that employers have a duty of altruism toward their employees. Armstrong is
an assistant editor of the* Objective Standard.

As you read, consider the following questions:

1. Armstrong claims that everyone who advocates a living
   wage wants what?

2. The author contends that what segment of the population is particularly harmed by ending up out of work
   because of minimum wage laws?

3. According to the author, what kind of moral rights do employers have?

The phrase in vogue today with advocates of minimum wage laws—laws forcing employers to pay employees more than they otherwise would—is "living wage." But, apart from laws mandating a minimum wage, this phrase has no referent in reality. And laws dictating minimum wages are immoral.

The So-Called Living Wage

To get a sense of how widespread are calls for a so-called "living wage," consider some recent news stories:

- Some fast-food workers are "demanding $15.00 per hour" for their work, and recently many such workers walked off the job to show they're serious. Some call that rate a "living wage."

- California legislators recently passed a bill raising the state's minimum wage from $8 per hour to $10 per hour by 2016. In this case, that is the so-called "living wage."

- "The Milwaukee County Board [of Supervisors] will take up a living-wage ordinance this fall"—the rate in this case would fluctuate according to "federal poverty guidelines."

- The District of Columbia considered (and rejected) a bill to force "Wal-Mart and other large retailers . . . to pay their employees a 'living wage' of at least $12.50 an hour."

The fact that no one can agree on what a "living wage" is—is it $10, $12.50, $15, or some other number plucked from the air?—indicates that the phrase is totally arbitrary.

If the phrase means anything in literal terms, it would have to mean a subsistence wage. But no advocate of the so-

A Violation of Freedom

The minimum wage violates the principle of freedom because workers are not permitted to work at less than the politically determined wage rate, even if they are willing to do so to get or retain a job—and employers are prohibited from hiring them. The minimum wage does nothing to increase the productivity of low-skilled workers. Indeed, it prevents them from acquiring the skills and experience they need to move up.

James Dorn,
"The Minimum Wage Is Cruelest to Those
Who Can't Find a Job," Forbes, July 22, 2013.

called "living wage" wants to forcibly reduce wages to that required for mere subsistence. Instead, everyone who advocates a "living wage" wants to force employers to pay workers more than they currently do. (Although minimum wage laws would be immoral in any case, the fact is that most people who earn the minimum wage don't supply the sole income on which their household is living, anyway.)

What advocates of a "living wage" are really after is an arbitrarily set wage floor—a legally mandated minimum that employers must pay employees regardless of all relevant facts pertaining to their businesses.

The Economic Harms of a Minimum Wage

The economic case against the minimum wage is well known and easy to grasp. If the government forces employers to pay employees more than their work is worth to employers, then employers will either refrain from hiring the potential employees or fire those who don't provide value in excess of the legally mandated minimum wage. Thus, one consequence of minimum wage laws is that many people—particularly the young and inexperienced—end up out of work completely and, of course, are therefore unable to gain work experience and earn higher wages in the future.

Moreover, when the government forces up the costs of doing business, affected businesses must either scale back their operations or pass along the costs to their customers. This means, among other things, that wage controls force people (including the poor) to pay more for the food, clothes, medications, and other goods and services they consume.

But the economic harms that minimum wages impose do not stop advocates of such laws or even give them pause. Why? People who advocate minimum wage laws do so not because of their economic beliefs but because of their moral beliefs.

The Moral Case for a Minimum Wage

The (allegedly) moral premise behind minimum wage laws is altruism, the notion that being moral consists of sacrificing for others. On this premise, employers have a duty to sacrifice their own interests for the benefit of their employees—and government has a responsibility to force employers to act in accordance with this duty. According to altruism, business owners who act to maximize their profits thereby act immorally and must be forced to operate their businesses (at least in part) in accordance with the duty to sacrifice.

But, as a matter of demonstrable moral fact, business owners do not have a duty to sacrifice their interests for the sake of their employees, and they should not be forced to do so. The owner of a business, having built it or bought it, owns the business; he has a moral right to run it in accordance with his own judgment; and he has a moral right to hire employees on voluntary terms that make sense to both parties, given their needs, goals, and circumstances.

Of course, to run their businesses successfully, employers must offer competitive wages that attract, keep, and motivate quality workers. Likewise, to keep their jobs and earn higher wages over time, employees must provide their employers with value for value received. Thus, voluntarily agreed upon wages create a win-win, virtuous cycle in which both employer and employee can profit more and more over time. If at any time either the employer or the employee thinks that the relationship is no longer in his best interest, he is properly free to terminate it (in accordance with the terms of their agreements).

If an employee wants to earn a higher wage, it is his responsibility to gain the skills required to negotiate a higher wage in a competitive market. An employee should not seek a higher wage through government force; he should seek it by earning it, by trading value for value.

The main thing standing in the way of an unskilled employee gaining the work experience necessary to earn an entry-level wage, and then a mid-level wage—and so on, as high as his skills can carry him—are the clearly crippling minimum wage laws. Far from being raised, all minimum wage laws should be condemned as immoral and abolished.

Periodical and Internet Sources Bibliography

The following articles have been selected to supplement the diverse views presented in this chapter.

Doug Bandow	"Immoral and Inefficient: The Minimum Wage and Government Sin," *American Spectator*, January 13, 2014.
William Bole	"Minimum Wage: Rare Case of Moral Consensus," *Tikkun Daily*, January 17, 2014.
Patrick Brennan	"The Inequality Fetish," *National Review Online*, June 22, 2012.
James Dorn	"The Minimum Wage Is Cruelest to Those Who Can't Find a Job," *Forbes*, July 22, 2013.
Yasmine Hafiz	"Religious Leaders Call on Congress to Raise Minimum Wage," *Huffington Post*, April 30, 2014.
Robert Kuttner	"Austerity Never Works: Deficit Hawks Are Amoral—and Wrong," *Salon*, May 5, 2013.
Mario Loyola	"How the Minimum Wage Hurts Poor People," *National Review Online*, November 22, 2013.
Tony Magliano	"Raising the Minimum Wage an Economic and Moral Necessity," *National Catholic Reporter*, February 3, 2014.
Ralph R. Reiland	"Obama's Inequality Baloney," *American Spectator*, January 27, 2014.
Joseph E. Stiglitz	"Of the 1%, by the 1%, for the 1%," *Vanity Fair*, May 2011.
Kentaro Toyama	"What Moral Philosophy Tells Us About Income Inequality," *Atlantic*, February 2, 2012.

For Further Discussion

Chapter 1

1. After reading the viewpoints in this chapter, how important do you think religion is to ethics? Draw upon at least two viewpoints to support your answer.

2. Srini Pillay argues that the moral network of the brain is often at odds with the fear and craving networks of the brain, and that this interaction of networks is crucial to understanding how individuals behave morally. Based on Pillay's argument, provide two examples of how certain unconscious fears or cravings can make an individual act in an immoral way.

Chapter 2

1. Identify the contrasting positions that Daniel Bor, Peter Singer, and Benjamin Brophy take on the moral status of the fetus. Which position do you think is most compelling? Explain your answer.

2. Barbara Coombs Lee draws a distinction between aid in dying and assisted suicide, only supporting the former. Will this distinction alleviate the concerns expressed by Wesley J. Smith? Why, or why not?

Chapter 3

1. Kathleen Hunker argues that individuals should have the right to abstain from professional or business activities that conflict with the ethical values they hold as religious people. Provide at least three examples that demonstrate how a religious individual's values might conflict with his or her professional responsibilities. Do you think it is justified for an individual's ethical values to take precedent over his or her professional duties? Explain.

2. Ed Kilgore suggests there may be a distinction between the conscience of a pharmacist who sells a drug that will induce abortion and a baker who sells a cake that will be served at a wedding of a same-sex couple. Drawing on this suggestion of a difference of degrees, is there an important difference between a doctor administering an abortion and an employer offering health insurance that provides for abortion? Explain your reasoning.

Chapter 4

1. Robert H. Nelson claims that economic policies are implicitly normative, making moral value judgments. Drawing upon the viewpoints of Joseph E. Stiglitz and Arthur C. Brooks, what moral values might be said to exist in our current economic system?

2. Ari Armstrong claims that the fact that no one can agree on an amount that constitutes a living wage indicates that the phrase is arbitrary. Does the author commit a fallacy here? What are some reasons why various localities might have different minimum wages?

Organizations to Contact

The editors have compiled the following list of organizations concerned with the issues debated in this book. The descriptions are derived from materials provided by the organizations. All have publications or information available for interested readers. The list was compiled on the date of publication of the present volume; the information provided here may change. Be aware that many organizations take several weeks or longer to respond to inquiries, so allow as much time as possible.

American Life League (ALL)
PO Box 1350, Stafford, VA   22555
(540) 659-4171 • fax: (540) 659-2586
website: www.all.org

The American Life League (ALL) is a Catholic organization that opposes abortion. ALL sponsors a number of outreach efforts designed to focus attention on individual pro-life concerns. ALL provides brochures, videos, and newsletters at its website, including the brochure "A Person's a Person, No Matter How Small."

American Society of Law, Medicine and Ethics (ASLME)
765 Commonwealth Avenue, Suite 1634, Boston, MA   02215
(617) 262-4990 • fax: (617) 437-7596
e-mail: info@aslme.org
website: www.aslme.org

The American Society of Law, Medicine and Ethics (ASLME) is a nonprofit educational organization focused on the intersection of law, medicine, and ethics. ASLME aims to provide a forum to exchange ideas in order to protect public health, reduce health disparities, promote quality of care, and facilitate dialogue on emerging science. ASLME publishes two journals: *Journal of Law, Medicine & Ethics* and *American Journal of Law & Medicine*.

Center for Applied Christian Ethics (CACE)
Wheaton College, 501 College Avenue
Wheaton, IL 60187-5593
(630) 752-5886
e-mail: cace@wheaton.edu
website: www.wheaton.edu/cace

The Center for Applied Christian Ethics (CACE) aims to promote and encourage the formation of moral character and the application of biblical ethics to contemporary moral decisions. CACE sponsors conferences, workshops, and programming on ethical issues. It produces a variety of resource materials, including audio downloads of lectures and the *CACE eJournal.*

Center for Bioethics and Human Dignity (CBHD)
Trinity International University, 2065 Half Day Road
Deerfield, IL 60015
(847) 317-8180
e-mail: info@cbhd.org
website: www.cbhd.org

The Center for Bioethics and Human Dignity (CBHD) is a Christian bioethics research center at Trinity International University that explores the nexus of biomedicine, biotechnology, and humanity. CBHD has initiated a variety of projects, including a number of conferences, consultations, and publications. CBHD provides numerous resources at its website and publishes the quarterly journal *Dignitas.*

Center for Character and Social Responsibility (CCSR)
621 Commonwealth Avenue, 4th Floor, Boston, MA 02215
(617) 353-3262
e-mail: ccsr@bu.edu
website: www.bu.edu/ccsr

The Center for Character and Social Responsibility (CCSR) is an ethics center that focuses on the education of teachers. CCSR consults with school leaders and educators from numerous countries. CCSR performs research and publishes the quarterly newsletter *Character.*

Center for Genetics and Society (CGS)

1936 University Avenue, Suite 350, Berkeley, CA 94704
(510) 665-7760 • fax: (510) 665-8760
e-mail: info@geneticsandsociety.org
website: www.geneticsandsociety.org

The Center for Genetics and Society (CGS) is a nonprofit information and public affairs organization working to encourage responsible uses and effective societal governance of new human genetic and reproductive technologies. CGS works with scientists, health professionals, and civil society leaders to oppose applications of new human genetic and reproductive technologies that objectify and commodify human life and threaten to divide human society. CGS publishes reports, articles, newsletters, and the *Biopolitical Times* blog.

Center for Journalism Ethics

5152 Vilas Hall, 821 University Avenue, Madison, WI 53706
e-mail: ethics@journalism.wisc.edu
website: http://ethics.journalism.wisc.edu

The Center for Journalism Ethics at the School of Journalism and Mass Communication, University of Wisconsin–Madison, aims to advance the ethical standards of democratic journalism. The Center for Journalism Ethics fosters discussion, research, teaching, professional outreach, and newsroom partnerships for analyzing ethics issues. The center publishes several resources on journalism ethics at its website.

Character Education Partnership (CEP)

1634 I Street NW, Suite 550, Washington, DC 20036
(202) 296-7743
website: www.character.org

The Character Education Partnership (CEP) is a national advocate and leader for the character education movement and is committed to fostering effective character education in schools. CEP focuses on defining and encouraging effective practices and approaches to quality character education and provides a forum for the exchange of ideas. CEP has many resources available at its website, including the publication "Eleven Principles of Effective Character Education."

Common Cause

1133 Nineteenth Street NW, 9th Floor

Washington, DC 20036

(202) 833-1200

website: www.commoncause.org

Common Cause is a nonpartisan, nonprofit advocacy organization that aims to restore the core values of American democracy, reinventing an open, honest, and accountable government. One of its key priorities is making government officials accountable for their actions under high standards of ethical conduct. Its lobbying efforts in 2007 led the House to create the Office of Congressional Ethics (OCE), and the organization was instrumental in lobbying for the passage of the Honest Leadership and Open Government Act. At its website, Common Cause publishes research, testimony, and press releases, including "Boehner, Pelosi Must Keep Ethics Office Strong."

Concerned Women for America (CWA)

1015 Fifteenth Street NW, Suite 1100, Washington, DC 20005

(202) 488-7000 • fax: (202) 488-0806

website: www.cwfa.org

Concerned Women for America (CWA) is a public policy women's organization that has the goal of bringing biblical principles into all levels of public policy. CWA focuses promoting biblical values on six core issues—family, sanctity of human life, education, pornography, religious liberty, and national sovereignty—through prayer, education, and social influence. Among the organization's brochures, fact sheets, and articles available on its website is "It's Time to Reject *Roe v. Wade* as Invincible Precedent."

Council for Responsible Genetics (CRG)

5 Upland Road, Suite 3, Cambridge, MA   02140
(617) 868-0870 • fax: (617) 491-5344
e-mail: crg@gene-watch.org
website: www.councilforresponsiblegenetics.org

The Council for Responsible Genetics (CRG) is a nonprofit organization dedicated to fostering public debate about the social, ethical, and environmental implications of genetic technologies. CRG works through the media and concerned citizens to distribute accurate information and represent the public interest on emerging issues in biotechnology. CRG publishes *GeneWatch*, a magazine dedicated to monitoring biotechnology's social, ethical, and environmental consequences.

Ethics and Public Policy Center (EPPC)

1730 M Street NW, Suite 910, Washington, DC   20036
(202) 682-1200 • fax: (202) 408-0632
e-mail: ethics@eppc.org
website: www.eppc.org

The Ethics and Public Policy Center (EPPC) is dedicated to applying the Judeo-Christian moral tradition to critical issues of public policy. Through its core programs, such as Economics and Ethics, EPPC and its scholars work to influence policy makers and to transform the culture through the world of ideas. Through its program on Bioethics and American Democracy, EPPC publishes the *New Atlantis: A Journal of Technology and Society*, a quarterly journal about biotechnology.

Ethics Resource Center (ERC)

2345 Crystal Drive, Suite 201, Arlington, VA   22202
(703) 647-2185 • fax: (703) 647-2180
e-mail: ethics@ethics.org
website: www.ethics.org

The Ethics Resource Center (ERC) is a nonprofit research organization devoted to independent research leading to the advancement of high ethical standards and practices in public and private institutions. ERC researchers analyze current and emerging issues and produce new ideas and benchmarks on ethics and ethical behavior. ERC publishes research, which is available at its website.

Genetics and Public Policy Center

Johns Hopkins University, Berman Institute of Bioethics
1779 Massachusetts Avenue NW, Suite 605
Washington, DC   20036
(202) 265-5180 • fax: (202) 265-5423
e-mail: gppcnews@jhu.edu
website: www.dnapolicy.org

The Genetics and Public Policy Center works to help policy makers, the press, and the public understand the challenges and opportunities of genetic medicine. The Genetics and Public Policy Center conducts legal research and policy analysis, performs policy-relevant social science research, crafts policy recommendations, and influences national genetics policy. Available at the center's website are numerous reports, testimony transcripts, and issue briefs, including "Prenatal Diagnosis."

Hastings Center

21 Malcolm Gordon Road, Garrison, NY   10524-4125
(845) 424-4040 • fax: (845) 424-4545
e-mail: mail@thehastingscenter.org
website: www.thehastingscenter.org

The Hastings Center is a nonprofit bioethics research institute that works to address fundamental ethical issues in the areas of health, medicine, and the environment as they affect individuals, communities, and societies. The Hastings Center conducts research and collaborates with policy makers to identify and analyze the ethical dimensions of their work. The Hastings Center publishes two periodicals: *Hastings Center Report* and *IRB: Ethics & Human Research.*

Josephson Institute

9841 Airport Boulevard, #300, Los Angeles, CA   90045
(800) 711-2670 • fax: (310) 846-4858
website: www.josephsoninstitute.org

The Josephson Institute is a nonpartisan, nonsectarian, non-profit organization working to improve the ethical quality of society by changing personal and organizational decision making and behavior. The Josephson Institute develops and delivers services and materials to increase ethical commitment, competence, and practice in all segments of society, including its CHARACTER COUNTS! program for character education. Information about CHARACTER COUNTS! and associated material is available at the institute's website.

Kennedy Institute of Ethics

Healy Hall, 4th Floor, Georgetown University
Washington, DC   20057
(202) 687-0360
e-mail: kennedyinstitute@georgetown.edu
website: http://kennedyinstitute.georgetown.edu

The Kennedy Institute of Ethics of Georgetown University is a bioethics institute. The Kennedy Institute is home to a group of scholars who engage in research, teaching, and public service on issues that include protection of research subjects, reproductive and feminist bioethics, end-of-life care, health care justice, intellectual disability, cloning, gene therapy, and eugenics. It publishes the *Kennedy Institute of Ethics Journal*, which offers a scholarly forum for diverse views on major issues in bioethics.

Religious Coalition for Reproductive Choice (RCRC)

1413 K Street NW, 14th Floor, Washington, DC   20005
(202) 628-7700 • fax: (202) 628-7716
e-mail: info@rcrc.org
website: www.rcrc.org

The Religious Coalition for Reproductive Choice (RCRC) comprises national organizations from major faiths and traditions and religiously affiliated and independent religious organizations that support reproductive choice and religious freedom. RCRC uses education and advocacy to give voice to the reproductive issues of minorities, those living in poverty, and other underserved populations. It publishes a newsletter, *Faith & Choices*, and various articles such as "Believe It: Religious Americans Are Pro-Choice."

Bibliography of Books

Malin Åkerström — *Suspicious Gifts: Bribery, Morality, and Professional Ethics.* New Brunswick, NJ: Transaction Publishers, 2014.

David E. Boeyink and Sandra L. Borden — *Making Hard Choices in Journalism Ethics: Cases and Practice.* New York: Routledge, 2010.

Arthur C. Brooks — *The Road to Freedom: How to Win the Fight for Free Enterprise.* New York: Basic Books, 2012.

Fred Brown — *Journalism Ethics: A Casebook of Professional Conduct for News Media.* Portland, OR: Marion Street Press, 2011.

Stephen Darwall — *Morality, Authority, & Law: Essays in Second-Personal Ethics I.* New York: Oxford University Press, 2013.

Ben Dupré — *50 Ethics Ideas You Really Need to Know.* London: Quercus, 2013.

Mark Johnson — *Morality for Humans: Ethical Understanding from the Perspective of Cognitive Science.* Chicago, IL: University of Chicago Press, 2014.

Christopher Kaczor — *The Ethics of Abortion: Women's Rights, Human Life, and the Question of Justice.* New York: Routledge, 2011.

Anja J. Karnein
A Theory of Unborn Life: From Abortion to Genetic Manipulation. New York: Oxford University Press, 2012.

Samuel J. Kerstein
How to Treat Persons. New York: Oxford University Press, 2013.

Richard Kyte
An Ethical Life: A Practical Guide to Ethical Reasoning. Winona, MN: Anselm Academic, 2012.

Patrick Lee
Abortion & Unborn Human Life. Washington, DC: Catholic University of America Press, 2010.

Barbara MacKinnon
Ethics: Theory and Contemporary Issues. Belmont, CA: Wadsworth/Cengage Learning, 2012.

Joel Marks
Ethics Without Morals: In Defense of Amorality. New York: Routledge, 2012.

Christopher Meyers
Journalism Ethics: A Philosophical Approach. New York: Oxford University Press, 2010.

Paul O. Myhre, ed.
Religious and Ethical Perspectives for the Twenty-First Century. Winona, MN: Anselm Academic, 2013.

Thomas Nagel
Mortal Questions. New York: Cambridge University Press, 2012.

Michael J. Perry
Constitutional Rights, Moral Controversy, and the Supreme Court. New York: Cambridge University Press, 2009.

Carol Rovane   *The Metaphysics and Ethics of Relativism.* Cambridge, MA: Harvard University Press, 2013.

Steven Scalet   *Markets, Ethics, and Business Ethics.* Boston, MA: Pearson, 2013.

Jason M. Shepard   *Privileging the Press: Confidential Sources, Journalism Ethics and the First Amendment.* El Paso, TX: LFB Scholarly Publishing, 2011.

James D. Slack   *Abortion, Execution, and the Consequences of Taking Life.* New Brunswick, NJ: Transaction Publishers, 2011.

Anthony J. Steinbock   *Moral Emotions: Reclaiming the Evidence of the Heart.* Evanston, IL: Northwestern University Press, 2014.

Bonnie Steinbock   *Life Before Birth: The Moral and Legal Status of Embryos and Fetuses.* New York: Oxford University Press, 2011.

Lewis Vaughn   *Doing Ethics: Moral Reasoning and Contemporary Issues.* New York: W.W. Norton & Co., 2013.

Stephen J.A. Ward   *Ethics and the Media: An Introduction.* New York: Cambridge University Press, 2011.

Cynthia Willett   *Interspecies Ethics.* New York: Columbia University Press, 2014.

Index

A

Abortion, 60
  after-birth, 85, 88–89
  American attitudes, 35, 39
  bans, 74, 80, 81, 89
  court cases, 63, 64–65
  global rates, 81, 83*t*
  laws, 74, 81
  medical/"morning after pill,"
    82, 126–127, 130, 131, 135,
    139, 144
  moral relativism, 89
  pain and trauma, 62, 67–70,
    74–75
  "partial-birth," 69–70
  personhood considerations,
    60–61, 62, 65–66, 73, 74–75,
    82–84, 87
  post-care, 82
  professional decisions/
    conscience objections, 120,
    126–127, 130, 131, 135, 139,
    144
  reduced, education and family
    planning, 82
  safety/danger, 80, 81–82
  special cases/unique moral
    quandaries, 60–61, 62, 66–
    67, 70
Academia. *See* Colleges and universities
Accountability
  bodies, 67
  financial industry, 171
  learned helplessness vs., 176
An Act Respecting End-of-Life Care
  (Quebec, 2014), 97, 98

Adler, Felix, 45
Africa
  abortion rates, 81, 82, 83*t*
  religions and secularity, 18
African-American rights, 36, 146
After-birth abortion, 85, 88–89
Aid in dying
  justified by accepted ethical
    principles, 96–100
  as moral and just health care,
    91–95
All's Well That Ends Well
  (Shakespeare), 28–29
Altruism, 187
Alzheimer's patients, assisted sui-
  cide and euthanasia, 103
American College of Obstetricians
  and Gynecologists, 69
American Conservative
  (periodical), 179
"American Dream"
  challenges, lack of upward
    mobility, 151, 171, 180, 181–
    182
  via free-market economics,
    175–176
American Economic Association,
  155
American Psychological Associa-
  tion, 69
Americans United for Life, 68–69
Amish, 35, 126, 133
Amygdala (brain), 56
Animals
  cognition research, 77–78
  consciousness, 75–77
  as food, 75–76, 78

Life ethics issues. *See* Abortion; Aid in dying; Assisted suicide; Atrocities, human history; Euthanasia; Personhood; Potential of life
Life support choices, 86, 87
Lithwick, Dahlia, 127
Little Sisters of the Poor (religious order), 143–145, 146
Little Sisters of the Poor v. Sebelius (2014), 143–145, 146
Living wages, 185–186
London Summit on Family Planning, 82
Lopez, Kathryn Jean, 88
Loving v. Virginia (1967), 64
Lung transplants, 104–105

M

Madof, Bernie, 168
Mardel Christian and Education stores, 137–138
Married couples
    contraceptive use, 63–64
    interracial, 64
    perceived threats to marriage, 127
McCloskey, Deirdre, 154
McDonald's, 179
Meat eating and animal rights, 75–76, 78, 126
Media sensationalism, 112
Medicaid, 182
Medical aid in dying. *See* Aid in dying; Assisted suicide; Euthanasia
Medical care. *See* Health care
Medical ethics corruption, euthanasia, 101, 113

Mencken, H.L., 33
Mennonites, 135
Mentally ill people
    euthanasia and assisted suicide, 104, 105, 106, 107–108, 110, 111
    life's value, 113
Mercier, Jean, 96–100
Metacognition, 71, 77–78
Meyer v. Nebraska (1923), 64
Meyers, Chris, 65–67
Middle Ages, 15, 51–52
Mifepristone, 82
Military draft, 117, 126, 145
Mill, John Stuart, 16, 154, 159
Millennial generation, 43
Miller, George, 179–180
Minerva, Francesca, 88–89
Minimum wage
    economic harms, 186–187
    laws are immoral, 184–188
    moral and economic case for raising, 178–183
Minority populations, personhood rights history, 88
Minors, euthanasia, 103
Misoprostol, 82
Monash University, 88–89
Montana, aid in dying, 94–95
The Moral Consequences of Economic Growth (Friedman), 161
Moral frameworks, 55
Moral justification
    abortion, 89–90
    euthanasia, 105, 113–114
Moral relativism
    decline of belief, 20–29
    main beliefs, 20, 27
    pro-choice justification, 89–90
    weakness of arguments, 27–29